AHEAD IN THE
COUNT

AHEAD IN THE
COUNT

One Baseball Fan's Guide To Career & Life Success

Michael N. Mitcham

ISBN-13 978-0692853139
ISBN-10 0692853138

Dedication

This book is dedicated to the loving memory of my mother, father, and brother; their spirits are with me always.

Contents

Foreword

Having Michael as my big brother has been one of my greatest joys and sources of strength since we lost our parents and oldest brother. I have always looked up to Michael and emulated his leadership skills, success strategies, and the conflict resolution techniques that have proved successful in my personal and professional life, and in my academic roles as professor and college chair. His no-nonsense, bottom-line approaches have proved effective time and time again. Michael and I have a special bond, unlike many siblings. We talk and text daily, exchanging stories, emotions, and strategies to negotiate office politics. We learned early on that "Life Is a Team Sport," and have been best friends, confidants, and teammates ever since. Michael's unyielding optimism, unparalleled work ethic, and genuine dedication to family, colleagues, and others are captured in this, his outstanding book for anyone wanting to get to "The Ninth Inning."

—*Dr. Michelle Mitcham*

Acknowledgments

Words cannot express my gratitude to my wonderful wife Renita, whose love, patience, and constant support have allowed me to pursue my dreams and write this book.

My life's greatest blessings are my brilliant children, Lauren, Rachel, and Brian; they are my inspiration, and the reason I had the confidence to share my story in these pages.

This book would not have been possible without the encouragement of my amazing sister, Michelle, with whom I have shared an unbreakable bond since childhood.

A heartfelt thanks to my outstanding editor Max Gordon and my brand coach, Marva Goldsmith, whose expert professional advice and assistance made this book a reality.

The Detroit Free Press

The Detroit Free Press

Detroit Hails Its Champion Tigers as a Symbol of the City Dynamic

Half Million Jam Streets for Series Carnival

League's Council Votes
Sanctions Against Italy

The Ford-UAW deal

Detroit Free Press

World Series edition

monday

metro final

Gr-r-reat!

Fans go wild over Tigers

The naturals win in maverick way

Detroit Free Press

METRO

WE WIN

City Goes Wild After Tiger Victory

AMERICAN LEAGUE CHAMPIONS
Detroit TIGERS

Tigers Avoid Welcoming Mob

The Champions Weep in Joy

Inside the Free Press

The Opening Pitch

L ike my dad, I've been a lifelong fan of the Detroit Tigers. While I've never played the game professionally, I've been an avid baseball fan since I was just a kid, so this narrative has more than a few references to the game. But you don't have to know a thing about baseball to understand my story.

I was born in May 1962 and raised in inner city Detroit, in a neighborhood of neat, two-story, single-family homes set chockablock on narrow lots. My family lived at 5905 Colfax Avenue, in a modest 1920 home that my paternal grandparents bought after migrating from Little Rock, Arkansas, and lived in until they passed away in the mid-1960s.

In many ways, the residential streets in the area are unchanged, with the original houses still standing, and now-mature trees shading the sidewalks that line both sides of the streets. It could be the setting for a movie about any small town where the major industry has long since moved out but the residents remain, stubbornly tending their tiny lawns and potted plants. But today, many of the homes on Colfax and its surrounding streets have fallen into disrepair, with peeling paint, sagging porches, and patched roofs. Too many have wildly overgrown lawns and boarded-up windows, their occupants forced out by foreclosures and other misfortunes.

My grandparents' house hasn't been in my family for decades, but the boom-to-bust story of that neighborhood—that city, *easily*—could have been my own. In this book, I share the story of how I managed to survive, and even thrive, in the hope that some of the lessons I've learned along the way might inspire and inform others.

———

In 1950, the decade before I was born, the economy was booming, and Detroit was still a boomtown. Between Motown music and the auto industry, Detroit was flourishing, with more than 1.8 million people, twenty miles of new expressways, and plans for a new civic center. The good fortune was not long-lived. Motown had gone Hollywood by the early 1970s. Rising gas prices and a growing preference for the smaller, more fuel-efficient cars built overseas led to a prolonged decline in Detroit's slow-to-change main industry. Even in the 1950s, not everyone shared in the city's success equally:

> Racial tension remained high in the city, after a tumultuous decade that included race riots in 1943. After World War II, African-American vets returning home did not find the number or quality of jobs that were available to their white veteran counterparts. As mayor, [Albert E.] Cobo neglected civil rights initiatives that would have integrated the city's African-American population with white Detroiters. Housing discrimination was rampant. Police crackdowns aimed at black communities were regular.... Three years after Cobo's death by a heart attack at age 63 in 1957, Detroit's population had dropped nearly 180,000 from the census peak in 1950 as young families left for nicer, less expensive homes in the burgeoning suburbs. It was expensive to buy a home in Detroit. Not so north of Eight Mile and west of Telegraph.[1]

———

1. Peter Gavrilovich, "Mayors of Detroit, 1950–2013," *Detroit Free Press*, September 15, 2013, http://www.freep.com/story/news/local/michigan/detroit/2013/09/15/mayors-of-detroit-19502013/77154478/.

Our block on Colfax consisted of a mix of working, unemployed, and retired neighbors, along with a handful of unwed mothers living on government assistance. In our lively neighborhood, children played in the street as well as in the back alleys, and we always had to look out for cars racing down the street. We lived less than a block from Warren Avenue, a major thoroughfare. Once, my friend Dink ran across the street from his house to play with me. In a split second, a car hit him. It was that dangerous. (Luckily, he survived and is doing great today.)

In July 1967, Detroit police raided an unlicensed drinking club on 12th Street and arrested more than eighty people celebrating the safe return of two local Vietnam vets. The crowd of angry onlookers swelled. Someone threw a bottle at a police officer, and the celebration turned into a four-day riot, with 43 killed, 1,189 injured, and more than 7,200 arrested. Despite an emergency curfew and prohibition on alcohol and firearms, more than two thousand buildings were destroyed in the confrontation between rioters and looters—a significant percentage of whom were white—and police, National Guard troops, and army soldiers.

The riot spilled into our neighborhood from Warren Avenue. I saw buildings on fire, grocery store windows broken, and things I could not comprehend, like my next-door neighbor Bernard running home with an armful of shoes he'd grabbed from a burning shoe store. To my five-year-old mind it was the perfect backdrop for playing war with the toy M16 rifle my dad had given me for my birthday just two months earlier that year. I was outside playing soldier when a police officer spotted me with the gun. He walked me to our front door and told my parents I wasn't safe playing with a toy weapon during a riot. My mother made my dad take it back and get me a toy boat. A black kid with a toy gun today? The police might well have shot me.

———

My mom, Birdie Almeta Nannan Mitcham

My mother, Birdie, was a Jamaican immigrant of East Indian descent. Her name suited her: she was a small woman, about 4'11" tall. Her parents, James and Jane Nannan, migrated from India to Jamaica in the early 1900s in search of employment opportunities. In those days, Indians performed manual labor jobs that most people didn't want. My mother gave me her maiden name, "Nannan," as my middle name.

My mother had a very difficult childhood. Jane died when Birdie was an infant, after giving birth to several children in a short span of years. James was a supervisor at a sugar cane plantation in Jamaica. On one frightful day, he caught two employees stealing from the company. When he made it clear he meant to turn them in, the thieves beat him with a pole to avoid getting into trouble for stealing. They were charged with murder when James died of internal injuries.

After that, my mother's older sisters, as well as her older brother and his wife, helped raise her. Birdie didn't like living with her brother, Egbert, and his wife, Doris. Doris treated my mother badly, making her clean the house and eat scraps and leftovers. She pleaded with her oldest sister, Adina, to keep her away from "bad" Doris.

My loving mother was a proud homemaker and a great cook. Her formal schooling ended after the eighth grade, but her education never ended. She enhanced her wisdom and knowledge by reading books, newspapers, and magazines, and watching news programs and documentaries. She was twenty-five years younger than my dad, Ossip Sr. My parents were introduced by my Uncle Orin and Aunt Louise, who had met through an international pen pal program. The two brothers, Orin and Ossip, married the two sisters, Louise and Birdie. Neither of my parents had been married before, and neither had had any previous children.

My father was African-American and born in Little Rock, Arkansas. He was passionate about baseball, fairness, and his family. He was of average height, about 5'7" tall, but I always looked up to him. After graduating from Northwestern High School and serving in WWII as a corporal for about five years, he worked for the United States Postal Service (USPS). When we needed extra money for the holidays, he delivered Chinese food in the evenings, and sometimes let us ride with him on those evenings. My dad was known for his generosity to family and friends and willingness to give the shirt off his back to help someone in need; for example, he gave his GI Bill benefits to his maternal cousin Wilhelmina, who was like a little sister to him, so that she and her husband, Edward, could buy their first house.

We were a family of five. I was the middle child. I had an older brother, Ossip Jr., named after my father, and a younger sister, Michelle Almeta; she and our mother shared the same middle name. My siblings and I were born two years apart, and we all grew up to be taller than either of our parents. We didn't have a lot of money, but we were a very happy, close-knit family.

———

That closeness, commitment, and loyalty provided a strong foundation for me. It's one of the main reasons I learned early on how to get back up when life knocked me down. It's the basis of my first life lesson:

Life Is a Team Sport

Much of what follows is structured by my work life and career, but don't let that fool you. I consider myself a success not for what I have done or what I have achieved, but for who I have become: a dad, a husband, a supportive brother, a reliable friend, and a good man. No matter what you do to earn a living, never forget to take advantage of any extra time you can find—*make time!*—to spend with your family, friends and loved ones. As Michael Jordan once said, "Talent wins games, but teamwork and intelligence win championships."

Early Innings

Growing up as a mixed-race person in Detroit taught me a lot. Throughout our lives, my siblings and I have lived with questions about where we're from. Asian and Indian people frequently ask if we are Hindu or Muslim. (It was only after I moved away from Detroit that I started to learn more about my East Indian roots and culture, though.) We were frequently asked, "Where are you from? What are you?" or "What are you mixed with?" I didn't realize we were any different from our neighbors until I went to school.

When my brother and I attended Sampson Elementary School, we always needed a teacher or other adult to walk us to the restroom or through the halls because girls tried to touch our hair. We three kids had the same straight, coal-black hair; even my sister's long hair had barely a wave to it. It was crazy: some kids in the neighborhood said we had white people's hair, but when we moved to Northwest Detroit, the white people there called us black, because our skin was brown.

I remember once in second grade, I overheard some classmates whispering. I leaned back and heard one of my classmates say, "He's a *nigger*." I wasn't familiar with the term. I turned around and asked, "Who? Where's the nigger?" They looked at me, shocked. They must have thought I was bold, standing up for myself—and not just genuinely clueless, as I was—as they said, "Man, you are *cool*." I smiled to hide my confusion. When I went home, I told my mother about it. She said, if they ever called me *nigger* again, I should punch them in the mouth. They never did.

I was tough enough if they had, but I was more comfortable with words than with my fists. When I was a young kid, my parents called me Huntley-Brinkley, after the *NBC News* reporters Chet Huntley and David Brinkley, for my tendency to report on anything and everything I'd seen around the neighborhood or at home. As an example, one day, our next-door neighbor Timothy, a twenty-something misfit, threw some rocks at our upper-level back porch. (To this day, I'm not sure why. I do know that he wasn't quite "right," and I suspect he had a secret crush on my mother and wanted her attention.) When my dad came home from his work driving a delivery truck for the United States Postal Service (USPS), he went out to relax on the covered front porch during a summer rain, and asked me to join him. Of course, he asked me what happened during the day. My mother hadn't told him about Timothy throwing rocks because she didn't want my dad to get upset, but Huntley-Brinkley didn't hold back: I spilled my guts and told him what the crazy dude had done. My dad marched into the house, grabbed his carbine rifle, and went upstairs to look out the up-stairs back porch door. Fortunately, he didn't see Timothy while he was that angry, or he might well have taken a potshot at him to try to teach him a lesson.

He wouldn't have hurt him, though. My dad was tough but fair. Of course, much of what I know about him comes from my brother's shared memories: I was just six years old when my father died in 1968, too young at just fifty-seven.

I remember answering the phone that morning. The voice asked for my mother. I heard her say, "The police? What kind of accident?" Then she paused, and urged us out the door to get to school. On the way, my brother and I mused over the word "accident," picturing it as just a minor injury, like a broken arm from a fall or a strained back from lifting—typical Post Office occurrences. Sure enough, when we walked home after school, there was his navy blue Pontiac Bonneville parked in front of the house. We ran inside to see him, excited to hear all about the accident.

He wasn't there.

Aunt Lou was sitting down, just hanging up the phone. She had a look of bewilderment on her face. She looked shocked, tired, and overwhelmed.

"Where's daddy?" Ossip Jr. asked.

"Yeah, where's daddy?"

She didn't sugarcoat the news. "He's dead."

My brother started crying immediately. I paused for a minute to process what she'd said and what it meant. My mother was walking down the stairs, holding my sister, with a solemn expression on her face. It seemed like I'd been hearing the word *dead* a little too often in recent months, but I still wasn't entirely sure if "dead" meant someone was gone forever, or just for a long time.

The city of Detroit owned and operated a transit system known as the Department of Street Railways (DSR) from the years 1922 to 1974. The morning of September 16, 1968, my dad was driving his postal truck as usual. He entered an intersection in downtown Detroit, where two DSR buses were parked in tandem, one behind the other. The second bus pulled into the intersection and collided with my dad's truck. The driver's side door slid open and dad fell out; he was crushed under his own truck. It was never determined who was at fault.

The year 1968 was a tough year for many people in the country. In April 1968, Martin Luther King Jr. (MLK) was assassinated. I'd seen him on the television before, and heard my folks talk about him with pride and admiration. My family and neighbors were in tears, and the shooting was a big news event, with lots of coverage in the papers and on the radio and TV. It seemed like people had just stopped weeping over MLK's murder when, in June 1968, Robert F. Kennedy (RFK) was assassinated, too. His violent death brought on more tears and shared distress, and once again dominated the news.

Is it any wonder, then, that when my father was killed just a few months later, my six-year-old heart and mind saw it as not just a personal tragedy but another staggering loss to the world? My world was certainly shattered, but others were also shocked and grieving. My dad's picture and obituary made the local news, and they wrote about him in the *Detroit Free Press*. Teachers, neighbors, family, and friends came by our house to express their sympathies. The government sent an American flag to cover his casket and arranged for a headstone for his grave.

My brother, who was eight, created a card out of construction paper, and on it he wrote a good-bye message to our father, saying how much he loved him and would miss him. He placed the card inside the casket, near the pillow, and the many visitors who read the card usually walked away in tears.

Ossip Jr. took dad's death hard; after all, he not only shared our dad's name but, as the oldest child,

My dad, Ossip Mitcham Sr.

he was the sibling who'd spent the most time with him—cheering on their beloved Detroit Tigers, playing catch in the yard while listening to games on the radio, like peers. Famously, less than a month after my dad was killed, the American League champion Detroit Tigers beat the National League champion (and defending World Series champion) St. Louis Cardinals, four games to three—their first Series win since 1945, and only the third in their history.

I thought baseball and the Tigers were "cool," too, but I was too little to follow the sport seriously or play catch, so my big brother—he was eight—followed the 1968 World Series because my dad would have, but we could all see that his heart wasn't in it.

For a while, the heart seemed to go out of all of us when my dad died. Later, of course, I understood that he hadn't been as famous as MLK and RFK, but that never changed my sense that his tragic, untimely death was a great loss to the world.

Ossip Jr., Michelle, and me

After being widowed at age thirty-two, my mother was left with three young children to raise on her own. She had never worked outside the home, and didn't feel she could once she became a single mom. She did have to learn how to drive a car, however.

When she received my father's life insurance payout, she bought a house at 19340 Coyle Street for about $25,000, and we moved to Northwest Detroit. She and my dad had always wanted us to attend private schools if possible, so she enrolled us at a Catholic school, Immaculate Heart of Mary (IHM), which we attended for the rest of elementary and middle school. (We returned to public schools for high school. Incidentally, IHM has since closed.) Since her only income was government assistance, the Catholic school required her to pay the entire first-year tuition up front, fearing—or perhaps hoping—that she wouldn't be able to afford it.

Why "hoping"? This was 1969. All across the country, affordable cars and the creation of the Interstate system had given birth to a new American Dream: the suburbs. White flight began with the prospect of lower-cost homes and expansive yards, but in Detroit it began in earnest after the riots of 1967, fueled by racist fears and changing realities like forced integration via busing.

The northwest area of Detroit became that city's new Promised Land, with fearful white buyers and hopeful nonwhite buyers moving out of the crowded city center, transferring millions of tax dollars from the inner city into neighborhoods that were already racially segregated. "By the end of [Mayor Jerome Cavanagh's] term, the city's population had dropped from 1.67 million in 1960 to 1.51 million in 1970."[2]

Although we were not the only nonwhite students at IHM, we were still a very visible minority. But within a few short years of our move, our new neighborhood in Northwest Detroit had transformed, becoming predominantly black, just like our previous neighborhood.

Our new neighbors, however, were generally slightly better off financially than those in and around Colfax had been. These people weren't as likely to be retired or underemployed; they were mostly aspiring, middle-aged workers looking for jobs in and around another suburban phenomenon: office parks, strip malls, and shopping malls, all with lots of free, easily accessible parking and a slightly wealthier clientele. Our household income of about $550 a month, however, hovered right around the poverty line. We qualified for food stamps, but mom was too proud to accept the assistance.

My mother could have filed a lawsuit against the City of Detroit since my father's accident involved a Detroit DSR bus, but she never did, partly because she thought filing a lawsuit might jeopardize the only income she had—a monthly Social Security survivor benefit

2. Gavrilovich, "Mayors of Detroit."

check from the federal government based on my dad's job with the USPS—and partly because no amount of money would have brought my father back.

Money worries may have played a part in my mother becoming very sick in 1970. She'd been going to a doctor who didn't seem able to correctly diagnosis her illness, and she was growing very weak and pale. The thought of losing our mother just two years after our dad's death was very scary. My brother, sister, and I prayed, teary-eyed, by her bedside every night, asking God to help her get well soon.

Finally, Aunt Lou took my mother to the hospital emergency room near her house in Ecorse, Michigan, where the doctors determined that my mother had internal bleeding from ulcers that had gone too long untreated. They warned us that she would likely die during the emergency surgery she required, and refused to operate on her. Not one to give up easily, my aunt took her to another hospital emergency room, one closer to our house in Detroit. That hospital admitted her and performed the necessary emergency surgery.

My mom said later that while she was unconscious during the surgery, our dad talked to her, and he told her that she needed to stay alive and raise the children. I've since read similar tales of near-death experiences in which the dying person speaks with deceased loved ones. Who knows what happened? All I know is that she had definitely been near death and that she believed his words kept her alive. She only told us that story after she had recovered.

Because she was recovering and because I already had very strong math skills, I took over the responsibility of managing the household budget that year. I was eight. My job included paying the bills, balancing the checkbook, and managing our household expenses, and I loved every minute of it. I recall my friends coming over and my mom telling them that I couldn't play because I was doing the bills. They didn't understand what that meant. (Over the years, you could see a visual history of how my handwriting evolved by looking at my writing on the checks.) Of course, addition and subtraction are only part of the skill set. I still didn't quite grasp the full context of personal finance, so if I didn't have enough money to cover all the bills one month, I threw one away, knowing that a new bill would be sent the following month. Handling the finances before I'd even hit puberty gave me a new level of confidence. While it was a very tough, perhaps even unfair responsibility for an eight-year-old child, the experience benefited me immensely, and I wouldn't change a thing going back. I am now an adult who's an expert at managing my finances—and I never throw away an unpaid bill.

In 1972, however, we hit a financial bump that my then-ten-year-old brain did not yet know how to handle, a potentially devastating financial crisis that might have meant losing our old house and maybe even our new one. When we'd moved in 1969, my mother had rented our old house on Colfax to a family friend. Three years later, when she received the property tax bill for our new house, she realized that she had not seen the annual property tax bill for the rental property. She decided to go to the county treasurer's office and find out the status, assuming it was just a clerical error. To her surprise, she discovered that the property taxes were delinquent, and the Colfax Avenue house was close to being in foreclosure. The property tax bills had been sent to the rental house, but the family friends living there never forwarded the bills to us or notified us of the monies due. My mother felt this deception was a deliberate action by the tenants, and she evicted them.

After the tenants moved out of the house, we went in to clean it up. We were still wondering how in the world we would manage to pay the delinquent taxes to avoid foreclosure. We were sure we would lose the house. Then, as we were cleaning up the kitchen, my mother noticed a loose board in the back of the wooden china cabinet. She jiggled the board a couple of times, wondering why it was loose. To her amazement, the board fell away, revealing a stack of US Savings

Bonds inside! My father had been saving them for years and had never told my mother. This unexpected cache provided enough money to pay the delinquent property taxes and keep the rental house out of foreclosure. We were incredibly grateful for my father's forethought, and couldn't help thinking that he was still looking out for us, even though he was no longer with us. My mother found a new tenant to rent the house, and thereafter she made sure that the county sent all the property tax bills directly to her at our house on Coyle.

———

Ossip Jr. and I were typical of most kids who grow up with little or no money: we did our chores and homework, played school and pick-up sports, and hung around the with other neighborhood kids. There were plenty of gangs in Detroit, mostly to the east and south of us, but we weren't involved in any of that. Our neighborhood was quiet, mostly untouched by the growing violence overtaking Detroit:

> In the 1970s and 1980s, [Detroit] became Murder City, and it was a title well earned. The murder rate peaked in 1987, with 686 homicides, or a rate of about 63 per 100,000 residents. The same year, New York City—the place where many Americans feared to tread—had 1,672 homicides, or a rate of 22 per 100,000. In its worst year, 1990, New York City had 31 murders per 100,000 residents, half of Detroit's peak rate.[3]

Ossip Jr., our friends, and I were definitely not gangsters. We weren't even hooligans, and just barely mischief makers: we got into a little trouble here and there, but nothing serious enough to warrant more than a spanking by our mom or, very rarely, a warning visit from the police. I couldn't be a gangster; I was too sensitive about disappointing my mother, and I tried to keep secret from her even the most

---

3. Scott Martelle, *Detroit: A Biography* (Chicago: Chicago Review press, 2014), 226.

minor kinds of trouble we got into. Looking back, I realize that some of the things that we did were wrong and even illegal—fighting, underage drinking, smoking marijuana, and occasionally stealing; we weren't immune to peer pressure. Everyone around us was doing the same things or worse, and not joining in would make you a "punk." No one wanted punks around. (Oddly, though we kids in the neighborhood were all doing the same things, our lives took very different paths: some died in their twenties, some went to prison, and some graduated from college and have enjoyed successful professional careers, becoming lawyers, bankers, or doctors. One classmate from middle school is even in the US Congress.)

Though I was determined not to disappoint my mother, or earn her wrath, I didn't always listen to her. Once when I was in the fifth grade, a friend from across the street and I decided to go on a bike ride around nine at night. That meant we'd be breaking our curfew, but we did it anyway. We'd ridden for about two miles west on Seven Mile Road when two teenagers on one bike approached us. They cornered us and tried to steal my friend's bike. I jumped in and started fighting, throwing punches while my friend rode across the street, yelling for help. When he took off, I was still whaling on the two bigger kids, but they must have finally decided I wasn't worth their time and left, climbing back on their own shared bike and speeding away. I rode home by myself in the dark, not yet realizing that I'd gotten a bloody nose and was covered in blood. When I walked in the house, my mother and little sister screamed, thinking I'd been stabbed. They reamed me out for breaking curfew and fighting, but my mom was so happy that all I'd gotten was a busted face and not a more serious injury; I got off easy, all things considered. We stuck to our curfew after that.

In addition to not wanting to break my mother's heart, there were a few other things that I think saved me from getting into any serious trouble when I was a kid. The first was that as the family accountant, I often had money on my mind. I knew my mom couldn't afford to spend what we had on extra clothes and things for us kids, so I spent a lot of time figuring out ways to earn my own money. I always wanted money in my pocket, so I worked a lot of different jobs growing up to get it. I shoveled snow for $20 a house. I also raked leaves, took out the garbage, and washed windows.

One year I came up with what I thought was a great hustle: I bought a pack of firecrackers in Ohio (where they were legal) for twelve cents a pack, and then I sold them in my neighborhood (where they were illegal) for a buck a pack. When I was fourteen years old, I told the manager at Gregg's Pizza that I was sixteen years old, and began cleaning up the restaurant. Over time, I learned how to answer the phone, as well as make and deliver pizzas. One year, I worked at a bowling alley. The summer after I graduated, I cleaned up a high school as part of a youth employment program.

Sure, I knew a few kids who tried to get their money by what they *thought* was the easy way—stealing, scamming, dealing, whatever—but to me it made more sense to work for it. It came easy to me to find a steady job with a regular paycheck. The pay from working at a bowling alley or a pizza joint might have been crap compared with what kids my age were raking in "working" for the Errol Flynns, a street gang in East Detroit, but the upside was that I didn't have to worry about getting shot or sent to jail. That just made sense to me.

I remember reading something Greg Mathis once said. Mathis was a Detroit kid born just two years before me. He ran with the Errol Flynns as a teenager, but then went on to become a prominent judge (with a syndicated television show). Here's what Judge Mathis said about the lure of "easy" money:

> The husbands and fathers of Prairie Street provided a jarring contrast that I never aspired to: They'd trudge home after a grueling

day's work in some dirty factory, lugging a lunch pail, looking
tired and bent down and smelling like machine oil.[4]

For some, the lure of the streets was too strong to ignore, and it only
got worse as jobs got scarcer: "Crime travels hand in hand with job-
lessness."[5]

The second thing that kept me from running wild was that I had
other outlets. I started playing football and baseball in eighth grade,
and I played football all four years of high school. I enjoyed watching
and playing the game. My coach in eighth grade told me football was
"legalized murder"—that I could hit people as hard as I wanted and
not get into trouble. I excelled on defense; my coach called me an
"animal." I played football because I loved the game. Even though I
enjoyed the game, I knew I wouldn't be playing in the NFL. I could've
tried to play college ball, but I suspected that it would get in my way
of getting an education, and that was more important to me.

Another game I enjoyed growing up was pool. Two of my neighbors had pool tables, and I learned how to play at their houses. I
begged my mother for years to buy me a table until she eventually
bought me an inexpensive seven-foot table. I played all the time. I
frequently played by myself, practicing and perfecting shots. I read
billiard books and wanted to be the best player that I could be. Naturally, I soon realized that I could make money playing the game that I
enjoyed. Over the years, I have played for money at pool halls and
parties, and I hustled during college for pizza money. Shooting pool is
a skill you never forget, though it may take a game or two to knock
the rust off.

That brings me to the third thing that kept me on the right path
through my school years, and my next life lesson:

---

4. Greg Mathis, with Blair S. Walker, *Inner City Miracle* (New York: Ballantine
Books, 2002), 11–12.

5. Martelle, *Detroit*, 226.

Know What You're Aiming For

It sounds too simple, doesn't it? But having goals helps you focus. My goal? I was determined to go to college. Like Mathis, I guess I'd seen my share of people lumbering home at all hours from back-breaking shifts (this was before much of the automation), and I wanted something different. I didn't want just a series of jobs; I wanted a career—something with my own desk, phone, and brass nameplate. I didn't know what I'd be doing, but I knew what I didn't want to do. The season is a marathon, not a sprint.

Me with Michelle and our mom

Breaking Balls

I n the fall of 1980, at the age of eighteen, I packed up my clothes and drove ninety miles west to enroll at Michigan State University. I didn't have any money, and I had no idea of how I was going to pay for school, but my mother always said we *had* to go to college. I believed this to be a nonnegotiable expectation.

It wasn't as though I was following in the footsteps of my folks or emulating a personal role model. If I made it through, I'd be the first person in my family not just to graduate from college but even to attend one.[6] I didn't have anyone to give me help or direction—not even my

---

6. The second was my little sister, Michelle, the youngest sibling. We both graduated from Cass Technical High School. I took her under my wing and tried to be a father figure to her. I helped her with homework, taught her how to ride a bike, and taught her how to drive a car, among other things. I looked out for her, letting boys know that they needed to treat her right. Michelle worked, went to school, and raised three children. She earned her PhD and currently teaches at Florida A&M University. She's an expert in multicultural counseling, family mediation, and counselor education. She facilitates trainings, workshops, and delivers keynotes at regional, national, and international conferences. Her empowerment strategies have been featured in magazines, newspapers, and television; she was once a guest on *The Oprah Winfrey Show*. We remain very close today.

high school guidance counselor, who seemed more interested in retiring than in giving me any "guidance" about choosing a school, a major, or a career path.

When I arrived to MSU that fall, I followed the signs for incoming freshman registration to the basement of a building everyone called "the pit." The room was packed with kids my age of every color and description, all waiting in very long lines, and all jumping with the same nervous excitement as I was. As I got closer and closer to the front of the line, I noticed that the other students were writing checks. I hadn't brought a checkbook with me, and didn't have any money. But how much could it be? My ignorance about the cost of a college education made me fearless.

Finally, it was my turn. The person at the table handed me an orientation packet, and then she asked the question I'd been dreading— the one about how I was planning to pay for everything. When I said that I didn't know, I half-expected her to laugh and tear up my application. Instead, she politely pointed to another line, and said that they could help me over there. "Over there" was the line for federal financial aid and student loans. Thanks to my unhelpful guidance counselor at high school, I hadn't known that those kinds of financial assistance were available. I signed up and they let me register. When I realized how much it was all going to cost, my knees were shaking, but I knew I was doing the right thing.

I was going to *college*.

Of course, I wasn't handed a blank check, and the cost of tuition and room and board staggered me, even then. But I'd been handling money since I was eight years old. I could handle this. And I did: to supplement the financial aid and student loans, I worked as a math tutor for minority students in the engineering program office.

After my sophomore year, I served for two years as a resident assistant in the dorm in exchange for room and board. In addition, I floated money on credit cards as bridge loans to help finance my college education: I began each summer with a balance owed to the university, so a hold card would be placed on my upcoming fall registration; I worked each summer to pay off the balance before the fall, the hold would be released, and I could register for the upcoming sessions.

I worked hard every summer to make sure I could keep up. During my first summer after beginning college, I worked at United Parcel Service (UPS) in Livonia, loading and unloading trucks. I did such a good job at UPS that they suggested that if I attended college locally at Wayne State University in Detroit, they would promote me to supervisor. That was an intriguing proposition; the money would have been great. However, I believed that completing my degree at Michigan State University would give me the best chance of having a successful career, and not just a series of jobs—that desk, phone, and nameplate.

One of the problems with not having a strong guidance counselor was that I wasn't sure how to go about choosing a major. I was a math whiz, but I didn't want to be a math teacher or a CPA, so what should I do with my head for numbers?

When I first entered MSU, I thought I would major in computer science. Personal computers were becoming more common, and I figured that a computer science degree would easily lead to a job. However, one day I was reading *USA Today* and saw a little sidebar that listed the top starting salaries for engineering graduates. I believe the top salary was around $26,000. I thought that was incredible! Electrical and chemical engineering majors were at the top of the list, so I decided that electrical engineering would be my major. I went to see my academic advisor to change my major. She asked me if I was sure; I said absolutely. Being an electrical engineering major opened up many new opportunities for me, like summer internships and permanent job offers.

I've since realized that the way I went about choosing my major was not unusual. According to sociologist Kim Weeden of Cornell University, numbers from the National Center for Education Statistics show that family income correlates closely with what college kids choose to study.

> Kids from lower-income families tend toward "useful" majors, such as computer science, math, and physics. Those whose parents make more money flock to history, English, and performing arts.... It's...consistent with the claim that kids from higher-earning families can afford to choose less vocational or instrumental majors, because they have more of a buffer against the risk of un- or under-employment.[7]

Going to college changed the trajectory of my life. It was an eye-opening experience. For the first time in my life, I was exposed to higher education and the extraordinary idea that I could develop an initial career direction rather than just look for a job. Education is one of the most important factors to a person's success, and it's becoming more so now that many unskilled jobs are easily replaceable with computers, machines, and robots. Even people who possess an innate unique talent or skill can improve their abilities through education.

College also exposes young minds to a wider world view. Attending MSU, and being on my own for the first time in my life, I learned about life outside inner city Detroit. I'd known, academically, that the world was so much bigger than the one I grew up in, but in college I could see actual proof. There were students from all over Michigan, the rest of the country, and the world. I met other work-study students from poor city neighborhoods and others from small towns and the rural countryside.

---

7. Joe Pinskar, "Rich Kids Study English," *The Atlantic* (July 6, 2015).

I also encountered people who'd grown up with advantages I hadn't even known about. One resident assistant friend invited me to her house for Easter dinner in Bloomfield Hills, Michigan. Her dad was an advertising executive for General Motors. I had never seen houses and neighborhoods so big and so beautiful; it was amazing. I couldn't believe that her neighborhood was only miles away from where I had grown up and lived.

And then there was the student who sat next to me in freshman calculus. She rarely attended class, yet she always scored in the upper-ninetieth percentile on her tests. Meanwhile, I attended class every day and studied hard, yet I struggled to break ninety percent on exams. One day, I asked her how she scored so well on her tests. She said she didn't attend class because she didn't want to miss watching her favorite soap operas on TV. I pressed her again to explain how she could achieve such good grades without even hearing the lectures. She picked up the calculus book we used in class and waved it in front of my face. She said, with a smirk on her face, that her math teacher in high school had assigned that same book in her classes in Warren, Michigan. I was shocked. I had never seen that book before, and certainly not at my high school, which, at the time I attended, was considered the best public high school in the city of Detroit.

College opened my eyes in many ways. For one thing, I was only just beginning to realize that I was at a disadvantage because of where I'd grown up and attended high school. I needed to play catch up and not let my slow start prevent me from succeeding. I needed to keep focused and as free from distractions as I'd kept myself in high school.

———

My mother had more than her fair share of tragic and difficult times in her life. She grew up without her parents, and then she moved to another country to get married. Her husband was killed in an accident after nine years of marriage. She raised three children by herself, with only meager government assistance.

After my father's death, she never married again. She did, however, have a few disappointing relationships over the years—two with married men who promised to get divorced and two with men who had drinking problems. Sadly, one of the latter introduced her to drinking alcohol, and in many ways, that was the beginning of her end, after a long, slow decline.

One summer night while still in high school, I picked her up from her boyfriend Charles's house. As I was stopped at a traffic light, I looked over at her. The back of her hair was glistening in the moonlight, as if wet. I touched it and realized it was blood. She said she had fallen. I took her to the emergency room, where she received a couple of stitches. Just as we were about to leave, she admitted that her leg hurt, too. I asked the doctor to look at it. She had a broken leg! The doctor set her leg in a cast, and she was finally discharged.

She didn't want to talk about it, but I suspected that she'd done more than just fall. She'd been planning to go visit her sisters in Jamaica, and this happened right before she was scheduled to leave. Her injuries caused her to miss her trip to see her sisters, and yet she was being mysteriously quiet about what had happened. I kept at her until she finally confessed that her boyfriend had physically abused her.

I may have been a demon at football defense, but for this I needed some help. I contacted an adult friend, James, from the old neighborhood. We were still close, and he was someone I knew I could call when I had a situation that needed taking care of—including teaching someone a lesson.

James came over the next day. We waited until my mother returned home from visiting with Charles. As Charles parked his car in front of our house that night in the pouring rain, I walked my mother inside. By the time I returned outside, James had pulled Charles out of his car and was beating him mercilessly in the street. James then got into the car and put it in reverse, planning to run Charles over. I stopped him; killing the man was not part of the plan. I just wanted to teach him a lesson about placing his hands on my mother. Charles came by the next day and shot at the house for revenge. There were several family members home at the time, but no one was injured. A few days later, he came by to apologize for everything; his jaw was broken and wired shut. He never touched my mother again.

————————

My brother, Ossip Jr., didn't feel ready for college, so after he graduated from Henry Ford High School, he completed Chrysler automotive school to become a licensed auto mechanic. He saw it as a decent job, something he could do with his hands that would provide good, long-term employment. He was hired at a Ford dealership, performing warranty repairs on new vehicles.

In 1979, he met a woman named Linda at a bar and they started dating. She was a few years older. When their relationship seemed to be going well, she suggested that they live together. That sounded good to him, so he moved out of our family home and in with her on the east side of Detroit. Within the year, they were married.

It didn't take long for him to suspect that he'd rushed into something that wasn't what he wanted. He discovered that Linda was mixed up in some "questionable activities"; while he never told me specifically what these activities were, he gave me the impression she was involved with drugs and prostitution.

On October 9, 1980, I was just a few weeks into my freshman year at MSU when I got a phone call. Late-night calls are almost never good news, and this was no exception. It was my sister, crying, telling me that Linda had called to say that Ossip Jr. was dead. I knew that I needed to return home immediately to break the news to my mother and figure everything out. I called Linda before I left, asking her what happened. She said calmly that my brother had shot himself. I asked her several questions, rapid-fire. I asked her where he'd shot himself; she said under his chin. I asked her how she knew that if, as she'd told the police, she wasn't in the room at the time it happened; she said that she'd been in the kitchen when she heard a shotgun blast in the bed-room, and that the police must have mentioned where he'd been shot. It angered Linda that I didn't believe my brother had killed himself. She argued with me on the phone. I ended the conversation, saying that I was headed to Detroit, and we would talk face-to-face. In a pre-vious face-to-face argument with her, she'd pulled a knife on me. I was mentally preparing for another heated confrontation.

I immediately began driving to Detroit from East Lansing. Unfor-tunately, my fuel pump failed on the way, and my car broke down in the middle of nowhere. It was pitch black outside, but I decided to save my car battery and only turn on the emergency flashers when I saw car headlights approaching. After what seemed like forever, a ve-hicle approached. By flicking on my flashers, I caught the attention of driver, and was relieved to see that it was the Michigan State Police. Help at last! But instead of asking if I had car trouble, the officers demanded to know how I had known they were coming up the road. I explained that I hadn't known *who* was in the car, and that I had just been turning on my lights when I spotted any vehicle heading my way.

It may be a coincidence, but in 1980, Detroit was one of the areas under federal oversight by a consent decree for its failure to hire nonwhite officers in numbers proportionate to the demographics. For whatever reason, the officers made this scared, heartbroken black man, just eighteen years old, spread eagle on the car so they could search me. Then they searched my duffel bag. They asked if I had a gun. The entire time, near tears, I explained that I just needed to get to Detroit because I had just learned that my brother was dead.

Finally, they reluctantly agreed to drop me off in Brighton—half-way to Detroit—so I could call for a ride. However, the whole time I rode in the back seat of the trooper car, they made me keep my hands on the top of the back of their seat where they could see them. I guess they thought I had a gun hidden somewhere. Finally, they dropped me off at a Big Boy restaurant, and I called Michelle and her boyfriend for a ride home.

My brother wasn't just dead, however; he'd been shot. No one wanted to deliver the bad news to my mother. Everyone waited for me to arrive from East Lansing to tell her. When I arrived home, my mother's first question was why I wasn't at school. I said, "Something very, very bad has happened."

She squeezed my hands and asked, "What's happened to your brother?"

I told her what I knew. She was devastated. It was the most difficult message I've ever had to deliver to anyone in my entire life. Ossip Jr. was her first-born child, and he was killed one day after her forty-fourth birthday.

My brother's wife, Linda, swore that Ossip Jr. had shot himself. I knew my brother well, and I knew that he would never, ever do such a thing. In fact, just a week earlier, he had confided in me that he realized he'd made a mistake marrying Linda, and that he knew it was time to come back home. It seemed awfully convenient to me that he was dead so soon after telling me he was planning to leave a woman he suspected of criminal behavior.

The police treated my brother's shooting as a suicide, saying that he had shot himself with a sawed-off shotgun. They apparently didn't investigate any other possibilities—including my theory, which to this day is that Linda, or someone on her behalf, shot Ossip Jr. in cold blood—and seemed not to be bothered by inconsistencies. They didn't seem concerned that the shotgun was too long for someone to hold to his own head and pull the trigger. They weren't bothered that the shotgun had no fingerprints on it afterward, and never even tried to explain how my brother might have miraculously wiped his own fingerprints from the shotgun after fatally shooting himself in the head.

I wasn't the only one who doubted the official ruling: a few years later, I ran into a man I'll call Keith, who had been one of the first officers on the scene. We'd grown up near each other in Northwest Detroit. Keith told me that when he'd arrived at the scene, even before he knew who the victim was, the crime scene seemed very strange and eerie. When he discovered the victim's identity, he was in shock, and did not believe that my brother had killed himself. He'd always suspected that foul play was involved.

After notifying my mother of Ossip Jr.'s death, I went to the morgue to officially identify my brother's body, but they told me there that Linda's uncle had *already* identified the body. I didn't care. I went to the funeral home. I told them that I needed to see his body, that I was finding it hard to believe that he was no longer alive, and that seeing him would help me. The funeral home reminded me that Ossip Jr. had been shot in the head, so the casket would be closed; if I really wanted to see him, it would have to be right away, as they prepared his body, and not at the services. They asked me if I was sure—I said yes, I needed to see for myself and to touch my brother one last time.

Ossip Jr. (left) *and me*

My mother had expressed a similar wish, but I convinced her that she would be better off remembering him as he was when he was living. I knew it would be a ghastly sight, something that would remain in my mind forever, but I needed what we now like to call "closure." (Back then, I just called it "saying good-bye.")

It wasn't easy, but I looked at and touched his body. He hadn't been shot through the chin, but in the side of the head! I could see where the shotgun barrel had left a burn mark above his ear. That was in direct contradiction to what Linda had told me about where he was shot. It also made it even less likely that he could have pulled the trigger himself.

Linda had all his clothes. I had to call her to ask for something of his to bury him in. I also asked for his auto mechanic tools and his red steel rolling tool chest. I wanted to pick them up and finish asking her questions, but she said she didn't want me to come over. She called the police and asked for a restraining order against me and my friend James, claiming that we had threatened her. I had argued with her, and hinted that my brother's death wasn't a suicide, but I hadn't threatened her; I just wanted to know the truth. She refused to let me come over and collect his things, so I gave the funeral home some of my own clothes to dress my brother's body. I didn't want him to be naked, even though it was to be a closed casket and no one would see him. I would know. It was the right thing to do for my brother.

My big brother and I had been very close. We often played together growing up and, since we were only two years apart, we had many of the same friends. We sometimes went to parties together and double dated. I found his premature death very tough to accept. At first, I was so focused on planning the funeral, taking care of everything at home, and arguing with Linda that I never shed a tear. I concentrated on taking care of business, and kept myself numb until the funeral. At the services, though, one of my cousins, the Reverend David E. Mitchem (same family, different spelling), was delivering the eulogy. David was also my godfather and one of my first mentors. It was David who told me that as a Mitcham, I had a responsibility to the family; there were some things that I had do, and other things that I should never do. I looked up to him and tried to follow his wise counsel.

My family gathered for the services at Oak Grove AME Church, all of us acutely aware that our close-knit nuclear family had now shrunk to three without my father and now my brother. During his eulogy,

David started off with the simple, incontrovertible truth that losing someone so young is a tragedy and…

That was all it took.

At that moment, the reality that I had lost my brother forever hit me. I burst into tears, letting it all out. I don't think I stopped sobbing for the rest of the service.

After the funeral and burial, when we returned home, I went downstairs to the basement for something. My brother used to spend a lot of time down there. That day, the basement felt unusually cold. As I descended the stairs, I felt a very strange feeling, as if someone were there with me. I walked toward the bathroom, and suddenly the sliding plastic door on the bathroom vanity popped out on its own, landing right by my feet. I have no idea why; I hadn't touched it. I half believe my brother was trying to communicate with me. I don't know what his message meant, but I think he was saying good-bye.

————————

Our family's losses—my father's death, my brother's death, my mother's disappointing relationships, living month-to-month financially—finally proved too much for my mother. Where once her drinking had been a temporary distraction from her life's pain and sorrow, now her drinking became a near-constant escape.

About two years after my brother's death, her boyfriend Charles died of a heart attack. She called me that evening, and I drove over to his house. I could tell he was already dead, but touched him to confirm it, and then told my mother that I would call for an ambulance, that they would do everything they could to try to save him. The ambulance arrived shortly. The EMTs tried to revive Charles, but told us at the hospital that it was too late. I'd already known this, but I needed her to accept that we did everything we could to save him.

His death was the last straw for her. She became very dependent on alcohol and her health began to fail rapidly. I told her during one of her rare sober moments that if she didn't stop drinking, alcohol would kill her. She said that was fine—she was tired of living and life was too painful. My mother also told me that if she died, I was old enough and capable enough to take care of myself and my sister, Michelle.

Over the years, I had tried pleading with my Aunt Lou and Cousin Vie for help. They were adults, and they socialized with my mother. I thought they would talk to my mother about her drinking and warn her, as I had, but they shrugged it off. They told me that I was a child and that I didn't know what I was talking about. They thought my mother was fine and that I was overreacting.

They were wrong. Michelle and I would sometimes throw out our mother's vodka or pour water into the bottle. We saw the number of empties. We saw how she stumbled and heard her slurred speech. We knew she was not *fine*.

We also knew that her reliance on alcohol was an addiction; she couldn't stop drinking. We tried enrolling her in some rehabilitation programs to help her, but she wouldn't attend them. She'd go out of her way to convince us she was okay, and that she didn't have a problem. When she began a drinking binge, she'd be very happy. When she stopped drinking, she'd be cranky and evil for the first day. By the third day, she'd be sick, but her mood and mental state would be returning more or less to normal.

Being sick included throwing up and her body being weakened. She sometimes threw up blood. She threw up so violently at times it tore the lining of her stomach. Even that didn't stop her. In another day or two, she'd be back to her normal self, but before long she'd begin her next drinking binge, and the cycle would repeat itself. I had watched the cycle repeatedly for nearly ten years. She'd even been tipsy at my high school graduation.

On December 12, 1983, my mother died of congestive heart failure at the age of forty-seven. Her liver had failed. I was twenty-one years old. After a recent drinking binge four weeks earlier, she'd become

very sick, and my sister called for an ambulance. My mother was admitted to the hospital. I drove down from college to see her in the
hospital about two weeks before she died. When I arrived, a pastor
was in her room delivering her last rites. My mother had not spoken
all day. The nurse suggested that I shouldn't touch her; she was yellow
with jaundice and had hepatitis. When I approached my mother, she
opened her eyes and spoke for the first time that day. She slowly
reached her arm up around my neck, and I leaned down and kissed her
cheek. She was my mother; nothing was going to stop me from touch-
ing her. She asked me where my sister was. Even though I didn't
know, I said she was at home. My mother asked me to take care of my
sister, and I told her that I would. Immediately after I left, she went
into a coma and was placed on life support.

Two of my aunts were split on what I should do next. Aunt Lou
wanted her removed from life support, believing she was suffering.
Aunt Gwen wanted her to stay on life support, to be given every
chance to recover. After a few days, a young doctor asked me what I
was going to do. He said he didn't think she would ever wake up, but
wanted me to go home and sleep on it and to give him my decision the
next day. He hinted that the other doctors and specialists were just
racking up medical bills, knowing my mother would never recover.

That night, I lay in bed, staring at the ceiling, wondering what to
do. In the middle of the night, the phone rang; it was the hospital. They
said the lining in one of my mother's internal organs had ruptured and
she had internal bleeding that could not be stopped. They encouraged
me to come to the hospital right away. My sister was home, and we
drove up there together. We didn't speak in the car; we were both trying to prepare for what we were about to experience. The hospital had
removed all my mother's tubes before we arrived. She seemed very
peaceful, like she was sleeping. We held her hands as she took her last
breaths. In the end, I was spared having to make the tough decision

about what to do with her life. It was decided for me, perhaps by a higher power.

After leaving the hospital, we stopped by the bank to withdraw some cash from our mother's checking account. We thought it was a wise decision before it was known that she was deceased; we had to plan a funeral. It was just before the Christmas holiday. We decided to schedule the wake and funeral on the same evening, and to just have the immediate family attend the services at the cemetery in the morning. We wanted to shorten the formal grieving, which included providing food and refreshments for family and friends coming over to express their condolences. While we knew that everyone meant well, it was too painful to discuss our mother's death. Our neighbors took up a collection and presented us with about $200, which was all the cash we had at that time.

Our mother had a small life insurance policy, which we used to cover funeral and burial expenses. In the summer of 1984, we sold the houses on Coyle and Colfax. While the mortgage balances were not very large, we were unable to afford to continue making the mortgage

Mom and me

and property tax payments. We split up whatever funds remained. I applied my share toward tuition and living expenses. We also split up the furniture, and my sister kept our mother's car. I was attending college, and Michelle was living with her boyfriend and his family.

My mother had been a big Detroit Tigers fan and enjoyed watching their games on TV. I once attended the Detroit Auto Show, and brought her an autographed picture from former Tiger great and Hall-of-Famer Al Kaline. It made her day.

I still think about my mother all the time. I always tried to help her, wanting to ease her pain so that she could be happy about life. The holiday season is a difficult time for me. Holidays were a special time for our family. We enjoyed watching the Christmas and Thanksgiving specials and parades on TV, drinking hot chocolate, and eating a holiday meal together. When she was healthy, our mom did her best to cook great meals for us and to buy us birthday and Christmas gifts. She taught my sister and me how to cook. Mother's Day is also extremely difficult for me. I always recognized my mother on this day, taking her out to dinner or buying her a small gift. If the song "Sadie" by The Spinners comes on, I immediately start crying because it reminds me of my mother. Even after all these years, the love in my heart and the pain of missing my mother has not changed.

Although losing my brother to a violent death and losing my mother to a preventable, but nevertheless heart-wrenchingly slow and inevitable decline and death, left me and my sister with an enormous void in our lives, in some ways it taught me yet another life lesson:

Play through the Pain

Just as I had when my father died, I grieved, then dried my eyes and picked myself back up off the ground. I don't know how I found the strength to push through the pain, but I thank my mother for showing me that temporary escapes like alcohol ultimately sap our strength and take away our will to live. It was not the lesson she would have chosen to leave me with, but I am grateful to her nonetheless. A champion gets back up when knocked down.

Leading Off

I spent much of my fall quarter of 1983 driving back and forth between East Lansing and Detroit to be with my mother and Michelle. Although I tried to stay focused on my college studies, by the time my mother passed away in December, my grades for that quarter were anomalously but hopelessly dismal. They were so bad, in fact, that I received a letter from the college of engineering, an academic warning: I needed to get my grades back up during the winter quarter, or I would be placed on academic probation.

I tried. I really tried. But although I wasn't crying or sitting in my room in the dark, I guess I was depressed. I couldn't focus. I had trouble sleeping. I found my mind wandering in class. Not surprisingly, I had another bad quarter and received another letter: I was on academic probation. This was my last chance.

The assistant dean of the college of engineering had signed the more recent letter, and I went to his office to meet with him and explain what was happening in my life. I wanted him to understand in case I wasn't able to bounce right back. He listened, nodding sympathetically, and suggested that I might want to consider taking some time off.

He wasn't alone in his advice; several people close to me suggested that I seek professional counseling or take a break to "get my shit together." The dean said that no one would think less of me if I took a quarter off or even longer, but he also made it clear that if and when I decided to re-enroll in classes full-time, I would need to get my grades up and keep them up, or I would be removed from the college of engineering. He recommended that I talk it over with my advisors, friends and family, and maybe the campus counseling center.

My life was at a major crossroad. This was a big life test and learning experience for me. I was at risk of failing to graduate as an electrical engineer, the goal I had set for myself as the first and most critical step along the path to a successful life in business.

I'm a believer, but I'd never been staunchly religious. Sure, we all went to church, and I'd spent part of my early education learning from the nuns at the Immaculate Heart of Mary Catholic school, but I hadn't spent a lot of time thinking deeply about God until that winter. During that rough period in my life, I reflected on why my family and I had faced such tough times. I thought about it from a religious perspective, and wondered why God would place so much pain and hardship on one family: my father's death, my brother's murder, my mother's addiction and death.

I'd heard people say that "what doesn't kill you makes you stronger," and for the first time, it made some sense to me. I thought about other people I knew who'd lost parents or siblings or friends, and about those who'd let life beat them down until they gave up. I thought about the people I knew who'd chosen the instant gratification and rush of drugs or crime over the sustained excitement of succeeding at something that took patience, perseverance, and dedication.

Yes, I'd grown up without my father's steady hand and sage advice, but I'd had a mother who loved me and taught me well. Yes, my brother had been murdered, and the crime had been passed off as a suicide, an injustice that still festered, but his death had taught me that every day matters—that not only do we need goals to pull us forward, but we need to appreciate, learn from, and make the most of every step along the way.

I concluded that there must be a God or supreme being who created the world; however, that God did not control people's daily lives or decide who experienced good and bad events. I decided that life is the miracle we are given, and the rest—what we *experience* during that life on earth—is based on our actions and the actions of others in the world.

My goal was to be successful in business, and in business, results are what matter. I realized that the result I needed was my education and engineering degree, and I took it to heart: I didn't take any time off. Instead, I registered full-time for the upcoming spring quarter and forced myself to focus. I achieved outstanding grades. In a surprise ending to that school year, I was nominated for and won a $1,000 Dow Chemical Marketing Development Scholarship. I also began setting my next goal.

Throughout my life, I've met good people who have been positive influences on me. (I've also known some bad people who have caused me pain and hardship. I've tried to learn from these life interactions, emulating the positive and shunning the negative.) Some of these positive influences weren't people I knew personally but were public figures I admired, like Muhammad Ali, Nelson Mandela, and Colin Powell, three men who faced and overcame significant challenges in life. They were all strong, charismatic leaders.

I also had many role models among the people that I knew and interacted with, and I tried to learn as well from the more personal role models. One role model was Kelvin, an upper classman I respected and looked up to. Kelvin worked with minority students in the engineering program office, and he explained to me the value that having an MBA degree would provide when combined with my electrical engineering degree. An MBA, he said, would position me well for a career in technology management, whereas a master's degree in engineering would be of real use only if I planned to pursue a research and development career. After speaking with him, I immediately set my next goal: I would pursue an MBA degree.

———

I graduated from Michigan State University in 1985 with a bachelor of science degree in electrical engineering. My Aunt Lou, my sister Michelle, and my cousin Cheralyn and her two kids attended my graduation ceremony, and we all celebrated at dinner afterwards. It was a proud day for our family and for me personally—a great accomplishment. I realized, too, for the first time that I would be a role model for others, including future family members.

By graduation day, I had already built a strong résumé that included three internships with General Motors and one summer internship with Proctor & Gamble. My first internship at General Motors was in the Parts Division. I helped coordinate replacement part orders for the enterprise. It was my first experience in a white-collar business environment, and I learned how to communicate and function with the full-time staff. At the end of the assignment, I had to give a presentation about what I learned. This presentation was given to the division's upper management, with a significant "prize": interns who made a favorable impression would be invited back for the following summer. My supervisor worked with me on the presentation. He wanted me to do a great job; my performance reflected on his leadership ability. The presentation exceeded my expectations. I was invited back the following summer.

My second internship at General Motors was in another department within the Warehousing and Distribution Division (formerly the Parts Division). This department was responsible for creating the parts catalogs. Traditionally, graphic artists and drafters created the annual catalog. I worked on a project that would create the catalog using computer graphics from the parts' CAD drawings. This made the catalog more accurate, and made it easier to modify any part as required. In many cases, no modifications were needed one year to the next, as those parts would already exist on a file in the database. Once again, I had to present what I learned at the end of the assignment. This presentation was also a success, and I was invited back for my last summer before graduating.

I decided that for my final summer internship, I wanted to experience a different company and industry. Working at General Motors had been a great experience, but I did notice that many of its employees seemed unfulfilled. Their jobs consisted of small steps in the overall process; their job satisfaction appeared low. However, they depended on the salary and benefits they received, and were willing to continue in jobs that were not totally satisfying. To broaden my experience and exposure to corporate culture, I accepted a summer internship with Procter and Gamble. I worked in the company's downtown Cincinnati headquarters for the consumer products company, where I was tasked with analyzing the power distribution system at the headquarters building. I worked with the in-house electricians to gather power readings. The increased use of computers, printers, and fax machines was consuming power that had not been anticipated when the existing power distribution system had been designed. At the end of the summer, I presented my findings and recommendations. This assignment and industry was very different from my

Hard at work during my internship at P&G

first two at GM, but once again, I received positive feedback and reviews of my work.

When I returned to MSU, I had one class to complete before graduation. General Motors had approached me about working during that last quarter at the Oldsmobile Plant in Lansing, performing an audit of their computer equipment. I decided to accept the opportunity to earn some money and work in a production environment. The assignment provided yet another unique work experience.

My various internship experiences taught me about life in a business environment. The three most memorable lessons:

- You must be able to communicate effectively, in both oral presentations and written reports.
- There can be trade-offs between job satisfaction and compensation and benefits.
- An engineer can perform vastly different jobs depending on the type of industry.

Based on my experiences in the automotive and consumer products industries, I needed to decide if they represented the type of work and industry I should pursue upon graduation.

———

Of course, I'd also added some character-building life experiences outside the classroom. For one thing, I'd spent two years as a resident assistant (RA) in a dorm. Anyone who thinks that's a piece of cake has never spent any time in a college dormitory. RAs are peer leaders, not just glorified babysitters.

I was attracted to the job initially because it meant I'd get free room and board and my own room. However, I soon realized that being an RA was a serious commitment that came with some heady responsibilities. It was also one of the best possible ways I could have prepared myself for my life in business and management—and in some ways, for parenting, too. The training is extensive, as RAs are responsible for dealing with all kinds of issues, situations, and occasionally crises. My training covered conflict resolution, resource management (learning about campus services like counseling and tutoring), teamwork, problem solving, setting boundaries, and diversity. I was well aware that I was an RA 24/7, not just when I was on the floor, and I had to set an example for "my" residents. Rather than making me self-conscious, that helped me focus on what was important, and ultimately gave me added confidence in my interpersonal skills and my ability to perform under pressure.

I remember one night when I ran into Pete, one of the floor residents, by the elevator. Normally a happy, energetic kid, that night Pete was drunk and depressed. Naturally, I was concerned. Pete seemed to be displaying suicidal tendencies, so I decided to stay with him until his condition improved. We sat on the floor and talked for what seemed like hours. At times, I hugged him and kept him calm. He eventually fell asleep for a little while. Once we woke up, he seemed back to normal. I felt that the crisis was over and I walked him back to his dorm room. It wasn't how I had planned to spend my evening, but in a 24/7 role, unexpected events occur. That was part of the challenge—and the appeal—of the job.

Another experience that helped me immensely (and looked good on my résumé!) was serving as president of the Minority Students in Engineering (MSE), a local chapter of the National Society of Black Engineers (NSBE). The NSBE was started in 1971 when two undergraduates at Purdue University decided to address the ongoing problems of retention and recruitment of black engineering students. During the late 1960s, some 80 percent of black freshmen engineers dropped out of Purdue's program. The organization went national several years later, and grew exponentially. The National Society of Black

Engineers (NSBE), with more than 30,000 members, is one of the largest student-governed organizations in the country.[8]

As president of the MSE, I coordinated a member field trip to the McDonnell Douglas headquarters in St. Louis. This was more than a decade after the landmark case of *McDonnell Douglas Corp. v. Green*, 411 U.S. 792 (1973). In that case, Percy Green, a black mechanic and

Minority Students in Engineering, the Michigan State University chapter of NSBE, visits McDonnell Douglas

laboratory technician, was laid off in 1964 by McDonnell Douglas during a workforce reduction. Green, who had been a long-time, vocal activist in the civil rights movement, claimed that his discharge had been racially motivated. The US Supreme Court ruled 9-0 in Green's favor. That ruling had obviously been a wakeup call for McDonnell Douglas (now owned by Boeing), as well as other companies in the

---

8. "MSU College of Engineering Scholars Program Recognized by National Society of Black Engineers and ExxonMobil," last modified April 20, 2012, https://www.egr.msu.edu/news/2012/05/16/msu-college-engineering-scholars-program-recognized-national-society-black-engineers.

United States.[9] McDonnell Douglas arranged for a bus to bring our MSE chapter members to their headquarters for a tour and meetings with recruiters. We spent the night and returned the next day, learning how committed the company had now become to developing a relationship with and recruiting minority students.

Today, the MSE has since been succeeded by the Michigan Louis Stokes Alliance for Minority Participation, or MI-LSAMP—which includes not only MSU but also the University of Michigan, Wayne State University, and Western Michigan University—and the MSU School of Engineering has its own Diversity Programs office, and "strives to be a community where people of different cultures, intellectual positions, and lifestyles can reach their full potential."[10]

Those opportunities allowed me to add leadership abilities to my résumé, in addition to solid work experience—and, of course, a degree in electrical engineering. At the start of my senior year, I started sending out résumés and interviewing for a permanent job. My Aunt Lou gave me $100 to buy a suit. I felt like an adult.

The first offer came from Procter & Gamble. They had been happy with the work I performed during my summer internship and offered me the position of engineer, for the General Offices, Corporate Buildings, & Real Estate division. If I accepted, we would discuss placement in one of the Technical Centers. It was my first serious job offer, an attractive salary of $29,100 per year, and—for the first time in my life—benefits like health insurance and paid vacation time. I'm still amazed that I didn't just snap it up out of shock. Fortunately, they gave me about sixty days to make my decision, during which time I had interviews with several other companies, including General Motors,

9. Angela Onwuachi-Willig, "When Different Means the Same: Applying a Different Standard of Proof to White Plaintiffs under the McDonnel Douglas Prima Facie Case Test," *Case Western Reserve Law Review* 50 (1999): 53.

10. "College of Engineering Diversity Programs Office: General Information," December 20, 2016, http://www.egr.msu.edu/dpo/about/general-information.

Ameritech, and even the Central Intelligence Agency (CIA). Should I take the job in case there were no better offers, even though the position wasn't exactly what I wanted? Or should I hold out for a better offer and a more engaging position? I could swing and go for an easy single, or I could risk striking out by waiting for a perfect pitch in the sweet zone that might never come, something I could knock out of the park. To date, it was the toughest work-related decision I'd had to face, and the pressure was enormous.

Then General Motors and Ameritech also signaled their interest in me, which gave me the confidence to decline the first offer. I was also intrigued by the CIA's interest in me, and I decided to attend the interviews at their headquarters in Virginia. (The sample security clearance questions alone were eye opening.) The CIA had discussed two potential positions that would make use of my electrical engineering background, one of which involved working overseas in an undercover capacity and would have prevented me from ever sharing information about my job with family and friends. I briefly pictured myself as "Scotty" in the *I Spy* reruns I'd seen as a kid, but ultimately decided that kind of life was not for me.

In the end, I decided to go back home to the Detroit area, accepting a position with a regional telecommunications company, Ameritech, one of the seven original "Baby Bells" created by the 1984 AT&T divestiture.

Ameritech (acquired by SBC in 1998) comprised Michigan Bell, Illinois Bell, Indiana Bell, Ohio Bell, and Wisconsin Bell. When the company's recruiter initially contacted me, I was surprised; I'd always thought of phone company employees primarily as the folks who climbed poles to string up the copper cable used in telecommunications, and that didn't seem like a job for a college graduate. Fortunately, instead of shutting him down, I kept listening. When he started describing fiber optics and data transmission to support computer networks, that piqued my interest.

My first role at Ameritech was as an engineer in the network engineering department. On paper, I was responsible for long-range planning of the fiber backbone network across the upper peninsula of Michigan. In addition to learning a lot about second-generation fiber optic communication systems, I was getting a serious hands-on education about the business. My district manager at Ameritech took me under his wing. He taught me the telecom business, as well as management skills, including how to be a better writer and how to develop and deliver effective presentations. He bled red ink on my reports and memos until I learned to write more clearly, concisely, and accurately.

I suppose I lived in a bit of a bubble, maybe because I was still feeling so blessed to have a job with a dynamic company, but eventually I became aware that many of my coworkers, especially women and other people of color, were not so enamored of him. They said he was biased and that he sometimes behaved inappropriately. I didn't notice anything unusual personally until one day when he and I were talking in his office. He said that I was different. He said that *they* typically look angry, but *I* didn't. At first, I just sat there, puzzled. I finally realized that he was referring to some of the other black male employees. I was shocked by his bigotry, but said nothing. How could this man who was mentoring me make a statement like that about some of my black colleagues? I changed the subject to exit the awkward conversation. I suspected that some of my peers had been visibly unhappy about the lack of promotional opportunities, but it was unfair to categorize them as a group of angry black men. They should be judged as individuals, with unique capabilities and experiences, just as I was being evaluated.

I remain grateful for that district manager's coaching, which helped me develop a strong foundation that positioned me well for future success, but I admit that I lost a great deal of respect for him that day. It reminded me that although I might have a great job, a nice suit, and my own desk, even my boss didn't see me as an engineer first but as a black man—a "black engineer" in the same patronizing, denigrating language as "male nurse" and "female doctor." It stung.

Maybe that's why I reacted as I did the night that my best friend, Cornelius, two female friends, and I went out to dinner to celebrate our new jobs and degrees. We decided to go to Carl's Chop House, Detroit's oldest, best-beloved steakhouse and a city landmark for more than sixty years (now closed, by the way). We went to dinner right after work, so all four of us were dressed professionally, in suits and business attire. We were having a wonderful time, and feeling hopeful: we were all on the way to living our dreams. The food and ambiance were excellent, and we laughed and enjoyed ourselves.

Then, reality. At the end of dinner, the middle-aged white waitress, who had provided decent service up until that point, dropped off the check. She looked at each of us in turn and slowly explained to us, as though we were aliens or rubes dining out for the first time ever, that it was customary when dining out to leave a fifteen percent gratuity.

My friends and I looked at each other, rolling our eyes, and continued laughing and talking. After all, we were all college graduates with professional jobs; we knew what a "gratuity" was and the expected amount. We let her patronizing attitude slide…that is, until the waitress came back a few minutes later and asked if we needed *help* calculating the tip! That remark was just plain insulting.

We asked to see the manager, and when he came to the table, I politely explained—my resident adviser conflict resolution training and experience paid off there—that while we'd enjoyed the food and had a good time, we'd been insulted by the waitress, and we would therefore be providing her with a *zero* tip. He apologized and asked us to please come back again for dinner in the future. We never returned to that restaurant.

That was in 1985, more than two decades after the Civil Rights Act of 1964 (Pub.L. 88–352, 78 Stat. 241) was signed into law by President Lyndon B. Johnson on July 2, 1964. That landmark piece of civil rights and US labor law legislation made it illegal to discriminate based on race, color, religion, sex, or national origin. But as recent events have reinforced, you can't legislate attitudes.

On a positive note, one of my best friends from high school was about to make history. Mike Wilson, who had graduated with a bachelor's degree in accounting from the University of Michigan in 1984, was appointed comptroller and vice president for the Detroit Tigers in 1988, making him the highest appointed African-American in Major League Baseball. He remained with Detroit Tigers until the team was sold in 1992. Another reason that I am an avid Tigers fan.

The life lesson of my college years and my first foray into the corporate world wasn't complicated. You might think that after all this—my stumble after my mother's death, my reaffirmation of my goal to be a success in business followed up so soon by the realization that many people would never see past the color of my skin—I'd grow bitter, more guarded. Instead, I realized the profound truth of one of the most commonplace, trite truisms I'd heard about life, work, and happiness:

Do What You Love and Love What You Do

I know that's nothing earth shattering or original, but it's true. If I'd been working a job that bored me silly or in a role that grated against my core beliefs, I might have let other people's small-mindedness crush my spirit. But I was following my dream and succeeding, or starting to, because I was working hard and enjoying myself while doing it. Engineering and science are not dry, dusty numbers in a textbook, but the stuff of life. I wasn't yet inventing anything or making critical discoveries, but I was being exposed daily to cutting-edge technologies, exploring new frontiers in communication, and getting paid for it.

Did that blind me to racism? Of course not. But it did make me resolve to be the best man I could be (*not* just the best "black engineer"), to keep trying to understand how others' lives formed their points of view (as mine had made me who I was), and to be the stronger person. As First Lady Michelle Obama said so eloquently at the 2016 Democratic Convention, "When they go low, we go high." Life isn't always fair, but sometimes you must accept what *is* in order to move on to what *can* be.

Put Me In, Coach

When I took the job with Ameritech after graduation, I rented a room from my Aunt Lou and Uncle Orin in Ecorse, about forty minutes away from my new job in Southfield. That made my daily commute manageable and allowed me to save money.

Though it had been three years since my mother's death, Aunt Lou still cried frequently, apologizing, saying she hadn't known my mom was so sick. The first month I lived in their house, she started to complain about a burning pain in her upper stomach area, and I half-thought she was just making herself sick with grief. When it grew more painful, though, she went to her doctor, who conducted tests. She was diagnosed with pancreatic cancer, and her doctors predicted that she had only months—maybe three to six months—left to live.

Aunt Lou left work immediately on disability. She made a final trip back to Jamaica to see her sisters, accompanied by my sister Michelle, who was pregnant with her first child. Even though I was working full-time, my next-door neighbor Ann and I helped my Uncle Orin care for Aunt Lou, turning her body to avoid bedsores and administering morphine for pain to keep her comfortable. Aunt Lou deteriorated quickly, and her rapid decline was very tough on my uncle.

Aunt Lou died six months after her diagnosis, in June 1986. After her funeral, Uncle Orin decided that he didn't want to live in their family home without her anymore; it was too hard. Instead, he wanted to move to Florida and live close to the ocean. He planned to sell his house, and told me that I would have to find somewhere else to live.

Before my uncle moved, I had a chance to take him to see his first Detroit Tigers baseball game. He grew up when the Tigers played at Briggs Field and blacks generally didn't attend the games. While sitting in the stands with other fans during a Major League Baseball game was pretty normal to me, it was a big deal for him.

Uncle Orin wanted to move to Florida before his house sold, so he signed his house over to me so that I could see to the necessary inspection repairs and manage the sale. I had hoped that I'd be able to work out a way to buy his house myself, but I didn't have nearly enough money saved by then. The move did get me thinking about houses though, and after searching around and exploring my options, I was able to buy a repossessed Veterans Administration mortgaged home at 16207 Stout in Detroit, less than fifteen minutes from Ameritech.

The narrow, red brick house was tiny and in need of fixing up, but that didn't bother me. My Aunt Gwen loaned me $5,000 for the down payment, and as soon as I closed on the house, I started right in with the repairs and cleaning. I did most of the work myself, hiring local repair contractors to help with the rest, but it didn't take long to get the house in good shape. My high school friend Phil, who was looking to live on his own, agreed to rent a bedroom. This arrangement worked out well for both of us. It was affordable for him and provided significant living space, and it helped me pay the mortgage. For a couple of years, we had fun living in our bachelor pad.

A few years later, my sister, Michelle, told me that she and her husband were breaking up, and asked if she could stay with us through the divorce proceedings. Naturally, I said yes. I'm her big brother. I helped her develop a life success plan for moving forward. My friend Cornelius was just completing law school, and he helped her file the necessary papers. One of the challenges in the divorce was managing to serve the divorce papers to her husband, since he was constantly moving back and forth between a couple of different states and was difficult to pin down. One day, I heard he was in town visiting his parent's house. I signed the process server form and dashed over there, serving him the divorce papers myself.

About that same time, in 1988, I was promoted from engineer to manager—a job change that would mean moving to the Ameritech headquarters in suburban Chicago. My sister couldn't buy my house and, in any case, she'd decided that she wanted to join my Uncle Orin down south, and finish her college education in Florida. I gladly accepted the new challenge and adventurous opportunity, and said goodbye to my first house.

Although I knew the decision was the right one, it wasn't an easy one, for two reasons. One, moving toward my new life goal, I had recently started an MBA program at the University of Michigan. Moving to Illinois would either postpone or change that plan. And two, I was in a relationship. My girlfriend, June, and I had been having fun dating, so I asked her if she'd like to move to Illinois with me. However, as the time for me to move quickly approached, she decided that we needed to be married before we could live together—that living together without being married would cause major issues with her parents. I was focused on my career and needed my personal life to be free of any drama. I sure didn't need any major issues! So, I said, "Sure, let's get married," thinking, *How bad can it be?* June and I went to city hall and got married.

We moved to Illinois in August 1988 as Mr. and Mrs. Mitcham. I was twenty-six years old. Two years later, I became a father, with the birth of my first daughter, Lauren. Until that moment, receiving my bachelor's degree had been the greatest thrill in my life, but when I held my baby girl for the first time, I truly understood the meaning of the word "joy."

––––––

In 1991, through Ameritech and Bellcore (Bell Communications Research), I attended a four-month mid-career program for employees, the Advanced Technology Innovation program (ATI), at the Information Networking Institute (INI) at Carnegie Mellon University in Pittsburgh. The focus was on new computing and communications technology, and how the anticipated advancements in hardware and software were expected to change our lives in the very near future. The INI was fitted out with NeXT computers (NeXT was Steve Jobs's post-Apple workstation company before he went back to Apple Computer and turned it into the powerhouse it is today).

Everything going on there was so leading edge—and, as it turns out, prophetic—that I walked around in a near-constant state of amazement. For example, we learned about an electronic billing system the INI was working on, a project that later becomes NetBill, that involved electronic patient records that could someday be used in hospitals and doctors' offices; now, in 2017, electronic patient records are a reality and are used almost universally in medical offices. So many of the things we learned about in the ATI program back then, ideas and concepts that seemed like something out of *Star Trek* or *The Jetsons*, have become reality today.

Soon after that program, I attended a seminar in which we were asked to document our career goals and describe what we could be doing to increase our chances of success. That seminar convinced me to go back and complete my MBA degree. I realized that while earning an MBA did not guarantee future success, it did eliminate a potential obstacle or excuse that could hold me back. I wanted to make sure that my job performance and academic credentials were as good as or better than those of anyone with whom I might be competing for a job or a promotion. That way, if I were not selected, I would at least know that it was not because of my job performance or qualifications. Tackling a new job, getting married, and having a second daughter had put the MBA on the back burner, but in 1992, I entered the executive MBA program at Northern Illinois University. After I received my MBA in 1994, I was promoted to the director level.

In 1994, I accepted an executive exchange assignment, working for Bell Northern Research in Ottawa, Ontario, Canada, for eighteen months. They were the research and development arm for Northern Telecom, a telecom-switching-equipment manufacturer that had a strategic partnership with Ameritech. The goal of the program was to improve partnering to increase speed to market. Although I was more than qualified, the opportunity was something of a divine coincidence, the happy result of an unplanned discussion—a unique assignment that I stumbled into by being in the right place at the right time. I was on a vendor trip, flying on a corporate jet with some Ameritech executives, when the topic of the executive exchange assignment came up. When they started brainstorming about who could take on the assignment, I volunteered. They were ecstatic—*and so was I.* That strategic assignment provided me with amazing exposure to the chief executive officers of both companies. Bobby Unser, former race car driver, said it best: "Success is where preparation and opportunity meet."

My family and friends were shocked when I said we were moving to Canada for eighteen months. That's the land of hockey, not baseball! But I viewed it as a rare, once-in-a-lifetime opportunity that I couldn't pass up, and I'm glad I did. I may have grown up just across the Detroit River from Windsor, Ontario, but despite its proximity to my hometown, Canada is a foreign country. More than one-third of the people in Ottawa, for example, speak both English and French. Fewer than 6 percent of its residents are black, but—even more interestingly—Canada doesn't label or classify people as "white" or "black" or even "nonwhite"; rather, they describe all Canadian-born people by such characteristics as primary ethnic origin (for example,

Jamaican).[11] In the 1990s (and into the 2000s), Ottawa was known as Silicon Valley North for its booming high-tech industry, especially in the field of telecommunications.[12]

Being in Ottawa for eighteen months gave me and my family—we now had two daughters—a valuable chance to view our country from a perspective of the other side of the border. It was a bit of a culture shock to live someplace where Washington, DC, was just another foreign capital (albeit a very important one), people were excited about the first-ever Tim Hortons Dragon Boat Festival, and when people complained about the Senators, they meant the NHL franchise team.

Living and working in Canada was like taking an extended vacation in a colder, older, more distinguished Disney park, where it seemed as though everyone was unfailingly civil even if they were angry with you. We returned to Illinois in late 1995, just months after two white domestic terrorists had blown up the Alfred P. Murrah Federal Building in downtown Oklahoma City, killing 168 people, injuring more than 680 others, and destroying or damaging more than three hundred buildings within a sixteen-block radius—the deadliest terrorist attack on American soil (until the 9/11 attacks) and still the deadliest domestic terrorism attack in US history.[13] As you might recall, within hours of the horrific attack, the news media were spreading unsubstantiated (and, as it turned out, completely unfounded and false) reports that "dark" people were responsible—specifically, Middle Easterners.[14]

Talk about culture shock.

---

11. "1996 Census: Electronic Area Profiles, Ottawa-Hull (Primary-Primaire)," Statistics Canada/Statistique Canada. Online at www12.statcan.gc.ca.

12. Guy Chiasson, "A View from Gatineau," in *Perspectives on Ottawa's High-tech Sector*, ed. Nickolas Novakowski and Rémy Tremblay (Brussels, Belgium: Peter Lang, 2007), 225–42.

13. "Oklahoma City Police Department Alfred P. Murrah Federal Building Bombing After Action Report (PDF)."

14. David Johnson, "At Least 31 Are Dead, Scores Are Missing After Car Bomb Attack in Oklahoma City Wrecks 9-Story Federal Building," *New York Times*, April 20, 1995.

———

From a career perspective, I now wanted network operations experience to help round out my background, work experience, and skills. (Continuous improvement is not just for work processes.) I had previously worked in planning and engineering, on T1S1 national standards committees, and had supported product development for residential and wholesale customers. After we moved back to Illinois and got settled in, I was able to land a key role managing high-capacity operations for business customers that utilized T1 and higher-bandwidth transmission lines—still at Ameritech—which would prove to be a critical experience in preparing me for future executive engineering and operations roles.

My life wasn't *all* work, though. I took advantage of the fact that I was in Illinois to connect with branches of the family there. I spent time with my paternal cousin Betty, who lived in Chicago with her husband, Roy. Betty was the Reverend David Mitchem's sister. She'd completed a lot of genealogical research on the Mitcham family, and taught me a great deal about our roots. For example, she explained that we have relatives (including her family) that spell our last name differently. Census takers in the 1800s wrote down their interpretation of your last name unless you corrected them; as a result, we have relatives with spellings of our last name on official documents that end in *am, em, im, eam,* and *om.* Intrigued, I also began collecting family information, and still have an active, growing family tree project; I conduct DNA and online research, but also gather information at the family reunions that occur every other year. Betty introduced me to the reunions, and it has been an absolute joy getting to know so many relatives. The family is perpetually fascinating in its variety, and includes doctors, lawyers, and educators, as well as a former NBA first-round draft pick.

Speaking of family, not long after returning to Illinois, I'd flown down to Florida to visit Uncle Orin. He was receiving chemotherapy for prostate cancer, and while I was there, I took him to one of his treatment appointments. The whole time, he fumed that he was done, that he didn't want the treatment. When the doctor showed up, I told him: no more chemo treatments. The reality was that Uncle Orin was not going to get better—the cancer had spread throughout his bones— and I wanted him to be comfortable and enjoy the time he had left.

Uncle Orin was grateful. While I was packing up to return to Illinois, he asked if he could go with me. It broke my heart. I knew the plane flight would be excruciating for him, and reminded him that I would be back in a few days. I was, but unfortunately, he passed away before I returned. I will always remember one day when I was a young child. I mentioned that something wasn't fair around Uncle Orin, and he snapped, "Boy, who said life was fair?" He was right about that. He died in 1996, ten years after his wife, my Aunt Lou.

I was only thirty-four, but between my uncle's death and my interest in genealogy, history, and my extended family, I decided it was time to make sure that all my family members buried at Westlawn Cemetery in Wayne, Michigan, had proper headstones: my dad, Ossip; my mother, Birdie; my brother, Ossip Jr.; my Aunt Lou; and my grandparents Sage and Burleigh Ann were all buried there. My aunt and grandparents didn't have headstones yet, so I worked with a monument company to purchase the three missing headstones. Uncle Orin wasn't buried there: he'd requested that his remains be cremated and to have his ashes spread at sea. My sister, Michelle, and I granted his wish; we spread his ashes during a family cruise in the Caribbean Sea.

Always Bring Your "A" Game

The lesson from this period of my life was sobering: the game only lasts so long. Eventually, the lights in the park go out, so it's important that you try your best to make every hit count, to field every ball. Run your fastest, and slide if you must. The best players make adjustments.

Free Agency

T he same passion for numbers and handling money that made me the household accountant at age eight never waned. During the 1990s, under President Bill Clinton, the United States enjoyed an economic boom that lasted almost ten years. I did my best to take advantage of this period of economic prosperity, especially through real estate deals; I bought and sold three houses in Illinois, taking advantage of the housing appreciation boom.

When I wasn't selling a house, I was refinancing a mortgage to take advantage of low interest rates. I only chose one-year, three-year, and five-year adjustable rate mortgages (ARMs). While most people viewed ARMs as risky, I saw the opportunity they provided. I monitored and adjusted my 401K contributions to keep pace with the robust stock market performance. I also exercised stock option grants, taking advantage of the company stock appreciation. While I greatly enjoyed the prosperity and the ability to save and invest for the future, I was also faced with the reality of climbing into higher federal income tax brackets.

What a terrible "problem" to have, right? Making too much money? In any case, my experience led me to provide a quote that appeared in a March 1997 edition of *USA Today*, advocating for a flat tax. I still think that while it's fair to pay more taxes as your income rises, the tax rate should not increase significantly. Pondering the complicated tax codes in this country made me I realize that I am a fiscal conservative: I believe in lower taxes, a simplified tax system, and balanced budgets. (I manage my personal finances to carry zero debt.)

However, I also realized that I am far from socially conservative. I have a compassionate social conscience. I was able to overcome a difficult childhood and go on to enjoy financial success in life, but not everyone could accomplish that without a little assistance—even more than my family had received. The poorer you are, the harder it is to climb up and out of poverty, and some people (particularly those with disabilities, chronic illnesses, staggering debt not of their own making, and those who for any reason have not attained at least basic language and math literacy) are unlikely to break free. For this and other reasons I remain more moderate on social issues. I don't believe in permanent welfare, but do support a short-term helping hand.

Trying to define myself with respect to the political spectrum led me to question my political party affiliation. It was clear to me that "Democrat" does not always equal "liberal," and "Republican" certainly does not equal "conservative," at least in the traditional sense of the words. I decided that I was an "Independent," and began supporting political candidates who shared my views on fiscal policy and social issues.

Independent: I liked the sound of that.

———

While driving to work one morning in 1999, I was listening to the messages on my phone. The CEO had sent a voice mail message to all employees, explaining that Ameritech had just been purchased by Southwestern Bell/SBC Communications (and would eventually be joined with AT&T Corporation) to become what is now known (again) as AT&T.

I had worked for Ameritech for fourteen years, and all my stock options would be vested at the change in control. I decided it was a good time to cash in my stock options and leave during the merger. I wanted to join one of the new competitive local exchange carriers (CLECs). *Hey, I was an Independent, right? I could do this!* I figured that if trying a new venture failed, I was young enough to bounce back, and life is too short to wake up with regrets. Besides, I kept hearing about former colleagues who had joined privately owned startup dot-com firms and were making lots of money on their initial public stock offerings (IPOs).

I decided to try it. I joined Birch Telecom, a start-up CLEC firm in Kansas City, Missouri, as vice president of engineering and operations. I was thirty-seven years old. I received significant shares of stock options that would be worth millions if the company had a successful IPO.

As the VP, it was my job to establish and oversee a department of one hundred employees responsible for the planning, design, engineering, surveillance, operations, and security of the local, long distance, and data networks. Initially, everything seemed to be going well. The company was well funded by firms like Kohlberg Kravis Roberts (KKR), and I hired some top-notch former colleagues and close friends into key roles. At one point, I was recognized in the Kansas City *Star*'s "Forty under Forty" annual list of rising stars.

Then came the 9/11 terror attacks in 2001 and eight years of the economic policies that resulted in a prolonged downturn in the economy and subsequent recession. Many companies went out of business. Many others were forced to reduce staff—including Birch. Now it became my job to terminate employees to meet financial targets.

Then I was "downsized," too, just three years after joining the company. Fortunately, I'd negotiated a severance agreement up front that would provide me with enough financial resources to get back on my feet. The planned IPO of the company stock never materialized; Birch Telecom was eventually purchased.

Even though I had taken a career chance that hadn't been a complete success, I wasn't discouraged. I learned and grew from the experience. I have always welcomed big challenges and long odds. As one of my MBA professors always said, "It takes risk and courage to redefine what is possible."

I was determined to not let this setback affect my family. By that time, June and I had three little children: Lauren, Rachel, and Brian. I was determined to make sure my job loss appeared invisible to them. I recall one of Rachel's friends telling her how sorry she was that her dad had lost his job, but the kids' lives never missed a beat. They never noticed anything different, except that I was working different hours for different companies.

I took a job working part-time at United Parcel Service (UPS) while I pursued new job opportunities. I started out working at night, loading trucks. It was the second time I had worked for UPS in my life. One of the attractions was that they provided even part-time employees with family health insurance, which allowed me to avoid paying expensive COBRA[15] premiums each month.

Working at night allowed me to be free during the day to look for full-time work and spend time with the children. Unfortunately, near the end of my shift one night, I crushed my left thumb in a work-related accident. Still, this painful challenge had a bright side, as during this time, UPS management realized the extent of my educational background, and promoted me to a supervisor position. I coordinated the conversion of all Mail Boxes Etc. stores to the UPS Store brand in the Kansas City metro area.

This may be a good time to share some of the things I learned while looking for another "real" job.

---

15. The Consolidated Omnibus Budget Reconciliation Act (COBRA) gives workers and their families who lose their health benefits the right to choose to continue group health benefits provided by their group health plan for a limited time.

One, remember that looking for a job *is* your job, and you need to approach it professionally, methodically, and enthusiastically. That means combing through all the places where jobs are listed (e.g., general job sites like Indeed, Monster, LinkedIn, etc.), as well as industry-specific job sites like (in my case) the National Society of Black Engineers. Reach out to all the resources you can, from executive recruiters and industry contacts to former colleagues and college alumni. Consider having your résumé professionally prepared.

Two, be realistic about what you want versus what you need. Consider part-time or consulting work in the short term. Don't let your desire to match or top your previous salary cause you to pass on a good career opportunity. While you're looking, learn what you can from phone and on-site interviews; this helps in clarifying what you want—or don't want—from your next position.

Three, remember that you're talking about a job, not a life-or-death decision. If a mistake is made, let it be your mistake, not a mistake from following other people's advice. And don't forget to exercise: it helps alleviate stress, improves your health, and gets your brain fired up so you can "think outside the box." Consider all options.

———

I was being considered for another manager position at UPS when I landed a position as regional vice president of engineering and operations at Cox Communications, a cable company based in Oklahoma City. Souchay, a former team member of mine from Birch Telecom, was a contractor at Cox Communications. When he heard about this open executive level position, he thought of me. I sent him my résumé to pass along. Before I knew it, we were moving to Oklahoma City. I was forty-one years old. This was a great opportunity to learn video, building on my knowledge of voice and data technology. It also meant another move for the family.

My family had lived in Chicago, Ottawa, Chicago again, and Kansas City. Now we would be moving to Oklahoma City with three kids, one of whom was almost ready for high school. Moving was hard on us all. I tried to spend any time I wasn't working focusing on the children—hanging out, taking trips, going to their games, performances, and matches—and loved every minute of it. My children were, and still are, my greatest love and achievement.

My marriage, however, was suffering. June and I had slowly been growing apart, to the point where nearly all we had in common was our children. We'd rushed into marriage for all the wrong reasons, and although we had both realized our mistake several years in, we'd stayed together for the children. We both knew the distance between us was increasing, but we never discussed it.

While my career was progressing well, June's had stalled out. After the new job she'd taken in Chicago upon our return from Ottawa proved unsatisfying, she stopped working in order to seek a new career path and focus on the children. About a year after she stopped working, she was diagnosed with multiple sclerosis, further complicating her plans to return to work.

In August 2005, I flew to Detroit for my high school reunion, while June stayed in Oklahoma. Being with old friends, laughing out loud unselfconsciously, reminded me that life could still be enjoyable. Several weeks later, I lay in bed, thinking. June was sleeping in the guest room. That was what we'd come to. It was not the path I had envisioned for my life or marriage, but it was where things stood. It was time to start discussing divorce. While I knew that would mean financial, social, and emotional upheaval—especially for the children—I knew it was the right decision. You can't put a price on happiness. I had avoided bringing up the idea of divorce, even separation, for years, afraid that breaking up would negatively affect the children. But the more I thought about it, the more I realized that raising children in a home in which the parents do not love each other and don't show each other affection and mutual respect isn't a healthy environment either. I reasoned that if we put the best interests of the children first, they should be fine post-divorce.

Initially, June and I were discussing an amicable, uncontested divorce. I was willing to be extremely generous financially. However, influence from June's family and friends soured our settlement talks and things took an unnecessarily contentious turn. June rejected my initial settlement offer and hired an attorney. I don't know what she ultimately wanted, but I likewise hired an attorney and rescinded the settlement offer.

When emotions take over, mistakes get made. Any settlement thereafter would be based solely on standard divorce guidelines. I was financially able to pay June an amount equal to half of the equity in our home, to buy her out without selling it.

Her attorney devised a plan to try and force me to sell the house. Selling the house was not a financial requirement; it was a deliberate move to take away something that meant a lot to me. In 2004, I had purchased 1.6 acres of land in Edmond, Oklahoma. I'd secured a construction loan and served as the general contractor to build my own home, hiring a builder who brought in subcontractors to build a house based on the modified architectural plans that I purchased. Since the builder was being paid a flat fee, there was no incentive for him to drive the price higher than necessary. The house turned out beautifully, and it had always been a source of pride to me since I was involved in building it from scratch.

We were both hurting. We both dug in. When I learned about June's attorney's divorce strategy, I prepared for a long, bitterly contested divorce if necessary. But in the end, we were both rational adults and we loved our children too much to tear apart our family with something so ugly. One day in the spring of 2006, June and I talked without lawyers present and reached a settlement agreement. She received half my assets, including equity in the home. I agreed to pay her rehabilitative alimony, based on an algorithm that factored in our years of marriage. Even though we legally agreed to joint custody, the children lived with me full-time, largely in deference to her medical condition. I took on the responsibility of guiding all three of our amazing children through high school and sending them to college while living in the house in Edmond.

––––––

One of the hardest life lessons I ever learned was that sometimes I could do my absolute best and still not get the results I was hoping for. You have to learn to accept that there are bad bounces. But when things look grim, don't break stride: push yourself. Remember:

Tie Goes to the Runner

That's how the game goes. Even star players get traded, but they never stop trying to get to the next base. Never give up.

The Bullpen

F orgive me. I just have to take a few pages to brag about my children. My marriage might have ended in divorce, but I wouldn't change a single thing if it meant not having Lauren, Rachel, and Brian. I always knew that I wanted to have children, when the time in life was right, and these three are the greatest blessings in my life.

Raising them has been therapeutic for me, too. I was not only able to give them much of what I never had as a child, but raising them allowed me to experience many of the things that I missed out on during my childhood. It allowed me to heal some childhood wounds and ease the pain that I carried for most of my life. Fatherhood made me a better person. I would not be the person I am today had I not been blessed with my kids. They affected my life as much or more than I have affected theirs.

Children each have their own unique personalities. I soon learned that it was important to allow my three to develop their uniqueness while guiding them in a similar direction forward, which included encouraging them to excel academically and participate in extracurricular activities like sports. Raising three children consumed most of my free time and was financially challenging. Academically, I set high

expectations for each of them. I made obtaining a college degree man-
datory; that message was engraved into them from the time they were
born. They each met and exceeded those expectations. Lauren earned
a bachelor's degree in business administration, an MBA, and a law
degree from the University of Oklahoma; she now works for a law
firm in Tulsa. Rachel was awarded a Morrill academic scholarship for
out-of-state tuition and earned a bachelor's degree in business administration from Ohio State University; she now works for a consulting
firm in Houston. Brian was awarded a Fry academic scholarship for
out-of-state tuition and room and board from Indiana University; he is
now completing a bachelor's degree in business administration from
the IU Kelley School of Business.

Brian, me, Rachel, and Lauren

All three children par-
ticipated in the gifted/spe-
cial education program in
their elementary and mid-
dle school. Admission was
based on IQ tests. I recall
when I asked the counse-
lor at Lauren's elementary
school in Kansas to test
her. The counselor told me
that Lauren was not gifted. When I asked how she knew, she said that
she talked to the teachers, and knew which children belonged in the
gifted program. I was certain that she was judging my daughter based
on her color and appearance, not by her academic ability and intelligence. I demanded that Lauren be tested; if she wasn't, I said, I would
escalate the request to the highest authority. The counselor reluctantly
scheduled Lauren for testing. A couple of days later, I received a nice,
very professional call from the counselor: Lauren had scored very high
on the IQ test, and was being admitted to the Gifted Education Program. It was 2002, and racism and racial bias were still alive and well.

I had tried to believe otherwise sometimes. When the girls were a bit younger, they asked me why some of the white students weren't always nice to them. I told them I would let them in on a big secret. I told them that some kids were jealous of children that were smarter than them. I told them to keep that secret, but to realize it may cause some kids to not treat them nicely.

In addition to the children excelling in academics, they played many competitive sports until the girls finally focused on tennis, and Brian on basketball. The girls played middle and high school tennis competitively and participated in regional and national US Tennis Association tournaments. Rachel was the Oklahoma High School Class 6A State Singles Tennis Champion in 2009. Brian played middle and high school basketball competitively, and participated in regional and national Amateur Athletic Union tournaments.

Engaging in competitive sports required significant time, travel, and money. We traveled to different cities and states for tournaments. Rachel one day asked me why I frequently was the only dad there with the tennis moms. I told her they were lucky to have a tennis dad. Both girls played in many of the same tournaments, which simplified some things. Brian usually joined us, and played with the siblings of the other players. As he got older, he attended summer basketball camps.

The girls' interest in tennis evolved indirectly from my mother's love for the sport. When I was a young child, before my mother began drinking, she had enjoyed playing tennis. Periodically, she and I would go to the park to hit tennis balls. We didn't keep score, but we did keep track of how long we kept a rally going. Afterward, she would frequently want her favorite treat, a Boston Cooler milkshake from Dairy Queen, made with Vernors soda and vanilla ice cream. I developed a passion for tennis because of my mother. Over the years, I made sure to always make time to play with friends, in tennis drills and lessons, and in some tournaments.

When we lived in Illinois, I played a lot of tennis. The girls' interest in tennis began when they were young, watching me play in tournaments. They always wanted to hit balls when the court was free, so I bought them tennis rackets and cultivated their interest in the game. I allowed them to hit balloons with tennis rackets in the house. They took lessons and, over time, began to excel, playing in tournaments when we lived in Kansas. When we moved to Oklahoma, I built a tennis court in our backyard, which enabled them to practice at home, in addition to playing at tennis clubs and in school.

People often ask me how I raised such smart and successful children. Every child possesses unique strengths and interests. The key ingredients in raising my children included setting high expectations, supporting and encouraging them to be well rounded, challenging them to strive for excellence, and trying to find the right balance between giving them space, and keeping them safe.

―――――

The skills that I used to nurture my kids are similar to those required to develop young talent in the workplace. There have been countless studies on the effectiveness of mentoring in the workplace. Not too surprisingly, most report that mentoring has significant benefits for the protégés.[16] However, I discovered that being a mentor also has benefits, including the obvious one of "giving back."

> Mentoring has been studied extensively as it is linked to protégé career development and growth. Recent mentoring research is beginning to acknowledge, however, that mentors also can accrue substantial benefits from mentoring. A meta-analysis was conducted where the provision of career, psychosocial and role

―――――――――――――――――――――――

16. Lillian T. Eby, Tammy D. Allen, Sarah C. Evans, Thomas Ng, and David L. DuBois, "Does mentoring matter? A multidisciplinary meta-analysis comparing mentored and non-mentored individuals," *Journal of Vocational Behavior* 72, no. 2 (2008): 254–267.

modeling mentoring support were associated with five types of subjective career outcomes for mentors: job satisfaction, organizational commitment, turnover intent, job performance, and career success. The findings indicated that mentors versus non-mentors were more satisfied with their jobs and committed to the organization. Providing career mentoring was most associated with career success, psychosocial mentoring with organizational commitment, and role modeling mentoring with job performance.... The findings support mentoring theory in that mentoring is reciprocal and collaborative and not simply beneficial for protégés.[17]

I have always enjoyed mentoring employees, as well as family and close friends. Early in my career, I had mentors who helped give me direction. These were typically informal relationships with executives that I established on my own. Without these mentors providing direction when needed, asking a critical question or challenging a decision, my career path might have been very different. I resolved from the start that mentoring would be one way I would give back to others as I advanced in my career.

I take the responsibility of being a role model very seriously. Successful minority leaders have an obligation to help others, especially the next generation. While I mentor my direct report employees, I have also made myself available to mentor other employees, and have been sought out for guidance by many women and minorities.

Minority employees always seemed naturally comfortable talking to me, most likely because they knew from my skin color that we had something in common. Many asked me directly to act as a mentor.

---

17. Aarti Ramaswami and George F. Dreher, "The benefits associated with workplace mentoring relationships," in *The Blackwell Handbook of Mentoring: A Multiple Perspectives Approach* (Chichester, Sussex, UK: Blackwell Publishing Ltd, 2007): 211–231.

One of the most frequent topics of discussions in these mentoring sessions was how to have a difficult conversation, like having a discussion with a supervisor to express their desire to reach the next level in their career. Many employees perform well in their jobs but aren't comfortable discussing plans to position themselves for a promotion. They often feared that they would be seen by supervisors as being dissatisfied, not committed to their current jobs, or overly ambitious. I worked with my mentees to help them communicate their career goals in affirming ways, encouraging them and role-playing conversations.

Often they would confide that they'd received performance evaluations that they found discouraging, confusing, or even unfair, and they'd ask me how they should approach their supervisors for specific feedback and to express their concerns. Many of my mentees wanted to know my story: how I reached my position, what obstacles I had overcame, and what personal advice and strategies I could share with them. In most cases, I focused on teaching them to build better relationships with key decision makers and to communicate more clearly with them. I helped many of them improve their performance, and helped others assess whether they were in the right role and whether they needed to consider changes in their career path.

One of my mentees was Patricia, a Hispanic executive at Cox Communications. Our early interactions in meetings revealed her raw leadership skills and long-term potential. We met weekly to discuss her development. The mentoring sessions covered such topics as how to handle an upcoming meeting, conflict resolution strategies, how to manage difficult employees, or how to respond to a specific e-mail or situation. However, one of our biggest topics was motivating her to complete her undergraduate degree. She was married with a young son, and going back to school was a daunting task. However, I finally convinced her that her lack of a four-year degree was a major obstacle, but one she could successfully surmount. It was the single biggest thing she needed to accomplish. I nagged her about it constantly, even after she had her second son, until she finally graduated.

I first met with Patricia when she was considering a transfer from our region to pursue a larger role; I met her for lunch one day to discuss a director-level opportunity in my construction organization. She was skeptical at first, but became more comfortable as we talked. The role had been held almost exclusively by white males in the past, so we both knew that there would be significant cultural challenges to overcome. Some might have said that I was taking a big risk supporting her for the role, but I knew otherwise: I could see her potential and her determination to be a success.

Despite skepticism from my supervisor and some of my peers, as well as pushback from some of her own employees, she went on to become very successful in that role. I continued to mentor her as she pursued a vice president role in another region, an effort that brought up the same concerns and doubts in others. In the end, Patricia was promoted and once again performed at a high level. The fact that she has continued to grow and excel in her career is a testament to the value and benefit of mentoring.

To borrow a phrase from Oprah Winfrey, *here's what I know for sure*…giving back is the fuel that has propelled my career. I once asked one of my direct reports at Cox Communications what he thought about me as a mentor (you can't assume that all is well). Brian, who was a director of business operations, said this about me:

> He's a real straight shooter and his door is always open. He empowers his reports to do their jobs, but is quick to provide support when needed. He is also not afraid to make a timely decision.

It's true that I'm a straight shooter. I'm also all about empowering others and that, along with the idea of "giving back," is what inspired me to write this book, in fact. It occurred to me that documenting my life experiences might be helpful to others, as many of the stories and experiences I'm sharing in this book are the same ones I would share in a one-on-one mentoring session, relating them to a mentee's current situation.

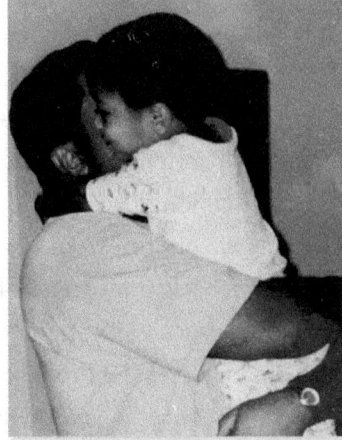

Top left: *Me with Lauren.* Top right: *Me with Brian.* Bottom right: *Me with Rachel.* Bottom left: *Rachel, me, Lauren, and Brian.*

———

Of course, parenting and mentoring are not the same thing, but they do have some shared characteristics. The main one is an important life lesson:

Be a Great Coach

Some people resist helping and training others, either because they fear competition or are afraid that any shortcomings they have might be revealed. But I believe we have a responsibility to prepare those who will eventually take our place to be the best people they can possibly be, and to smooth their way forward. The only way to sustain progress and improve on today is to help those who will lead tomorrow. Pay it forward.

Renita and me

Changeup

When I was eighteen years old, I was standing in my driveway. Across the street, I saw a girl who was visiting my neighbor, and—just like in cartoons—I felt my heart jump out of my chest. I immediately wanted to know who she was and everything about her. Eventually, I found a way to meet her. Her name was Renita. Sure enough, I liked her and wanted to ask her out. However, a good friend of mine, Derek, told me that she was dating older, more successful guys and wouldn't be interested in me. Based on his advice, I decided she and I should just be friends; that way, I could avoid rejection and maybe one day become *more* than friends.

Of course, our lives went in different directions for many years, and we never became more than friends. When I found myself single at the age of forty-four, however, I decided to find out where she was, and if she was married. I vowed that if Renita was still single, I was finally going to ask her out. I called a mutual friend to get her phone number. Unfortunately, the mutual friend accidentally transposed the last two numbers when giving the number to me, and I couldn't get through. Undeterred, I went on the Internet, did a search, and found her home number. She was living in Dallas.

I called and left a message. Renita called me back in about twenty minutes. We had a nice conversation. I invited her to visit me in Oklahoma City, and to attend a Los Angeles Lakers–New Orleans Hornets basketball game, along with the kids and me (the Hornets played in OKC for two seasons after Hurricane Katrina). Renita and I had floor seats, while the kids sat in the company suite. After the game, we went out to dinner before returning to my home, where we talked for hours. When I told her how I'd felt about her for the last twenty-five years, she shook her head. She said my friend had been wrong about her twenty-five years ago: she would have gone out with me if I had asked her!

Our relationship grew, and eventually she moved in with us. We got married on October 18, 2008, in Las Colinas, Texas. I was forty-six. We honeymooned in Ocho Rios, Jamaica, a country that has always been special to me because it's the birthplace of my mother.

Renita and me

With Renita, I finally knew what being in a happy, loving relationship felt like. She made me want to be the best person I could be. Would it have been the same if we'd dated back in high school? Who knows? Maybe this was the right stage in life for us to get together.

Married life with two teenage daughters and a preteen son was hectic, but happy. The kids accepted Renita into the family, and she has been very good with and for the children. It felt good being in a happy and loving relationship.

It was also a game changer. It energized me. In 2008–2009, I completed the National Association for Multi-Ethnicity in Communications (NAMIC) executive leadership development program (ELDP) at

UCLA. Founded in 1980, NAMIC is like the National Society of Black Engineers for the communications industry, and educates, advocates, and empowers for multiethnic diversity in the communications industry. They provide resources to allow members to cultivate their individual careers, and they partner with leading media companies that consider diversity to be a business imperative. The ELDP reaches out to upper- to mid-level executives of color on track for senior executive positions. Specifically, they "help identify and nurture high-potential executives of color; build and strengthen their skills, preparing them for promotion to more senior positions; provide useful tools to help them meet the unique challenges that confront professionals of color who occupy key leadership roles; and assist industry companies' retention efforts for executives of color."[18]

At the ELDP, I met minority professionals from across the country who worked in different areas of communications—cable providers like Time Warner, Charter, and Comcast, and programmers like ESPN, Disney, and Viacom/BET. It was an awesome experience to be in a class with so many sharp, high-potential minority professionals in an industry that I had been a part of for twenty years. The ELDP was like an MBA refresher; we covered all aspects of the business. The professors were from top universities across the country. We all left the program charged up, with our business skills sharpened, ready to conquer the industry!

Exciting things were happening in DC, too. Renita and I wanted to find a way to participate in the historic events that were taking place, to attend the inauguration of the first African-American president, but didn't know how we could obtain tickets. It wasn't as though we were on close speaking terms with new president-elect. I thought about it, though, and believed that very few Oklahomans would be seeking tickets, so I decided to contact Senator Tom Coburn's office. They

---

18. NAMIC, "About NAMIC," http://namic.com/dev/eldp/.

were happy to provide me with two tickets; we just had to pick them up from his office in Washington, DC.

So it was that on a cold day in January 2009, Renita and I stood on a train to travel from our hotel in Virginia to the Capitol and then stood all day in the cold weather to witness history in the making. It was an exhausting but proud day for America, and we were there. We witnessed the inauguration in which Barack Obama became the forty-fourth president of the United States, and the nation's first African-American president.

In April 2010, we attended the Reflections of Hope Dinner in Oklahoma City, as the Oklahoma City National Memorial and Museum honored President Bill Clinton for his work in helping transform Oklahoma City following the bombing of the Murrah Federal Building in 1995, and for his international peace work during and after his presidency. After the dinner, President Clinton made himself available to talk and take pictures with anyone who wanted to meet him, and Renita and I talked with the former president. He was so patient and willing to talk to us, very down to earth. It was an amazing, unforgettable experience.

The kids weren't excluded from the fun. Teenagers typically want to spend most of their time with friends, but we were able to hang out with them. We spent a few Christmas holidays traveling, spending one holiday in Jamaica, one in Hawaii, one on a Caribbean cruise, and one in Arizona. In 2007, we were the guests of the Oklahoma City Hornets for their game in Memphis against the Grizzlies; we flew with the team on their private jet from OKC to Memphis. The players were very welcoming, especially Chris Paul. We stayed in the same hotel as the coaches and the team and went on a tour of Memphis and dinner the next day, before attending the game. We flew back to OKC with the team after the game. It was an experience we'll never forget.

———

I am not the first person to hit forty and wake up feeling decades older. Somehow, I'd reached a point where I needed to lose about fifty pounds to reach a healthy weight and to feel good about my appearance. That sort of thing sneaks up on you if you don't live your whole life realizing that eating healthy and exercising regularly are as important as breathing. Determined to make up for lost time (and gained pounds), I began a regular exercise routine, exercising three to seven times a week. This helped my fitness, helped burn calories, and relieved mental stress.

I also started paying more attention to the caloric, protein, and fat content of my meals. I reduced my daily intake, and began eating high-protein, low-carbohydrate meals. One of the easiest changes I made was to stop drinking soda and sweet tea, reducing my sugar intake. I finally admitted that going to the doctor for regular check-ups is also very important—something a lot of men disdain—as is being happy about life. As I took better care of myself, I was better able to maintain a healthy weight, manage stress, keep my cholesterol and blood pressure at healthy levels, and maintain good energy and stamina.

For several years, I had ignored a nagging pain in my left knee. I finally decided to address that in November 2007. I had knee surgery that included a lateral release of the tendon. Renita, my nurse at home, helped me to recover. She has said I was a very difficult patient. I wanted to get moving immediately; I fell after returning home from the surgery and busted the stitches in my knee. After successfully completing physical therapy, my knee felt better than ever. I am not sure why I procrastinated getting it fixed for so long. Life is too short to be in discomfort, or to be unable to enjoy yourself because of your physical condition.

Except for pickup games, I didn't play sports anymore, but I was still an avid fan, especially of my beloved Detroit Tigers. After we were married, I introduced Renita to major league baseball. She had always enjoyed sports, but had been primarily focused on football and basketball. Once she started following baseball, she discovered that she enjoyed it and became a huge Detroit Tigers fan, just like me and my folks. She and I started attending games, sometimes traveling to see them play. One of our favorite movies is *For Love of the Game*, a story about an aging Detroit Tigers pitcher thinking about his emotional and physical limits—pondering life, his estranged girlfriend, and risk—in the middle of pitching a perfect game against the New York Yankees.

In October 2012, I managed to get two tickets to the World Series in Detroit so we could go and root for the Tigers. We loved every minute of it, even though it was so cold you could see your breath—and the Tigers lost.

Living in Oklahoma City, we were also able to attend several OKC Thunder basketball games. We frequently took the kids and their friends with us to those. Attending Game One of the NBA Finals in 2012 was an awesome experience; Brian even met ESPN sports personality Stephen A. Smith. (Unfortunately, the Thunder lost the series to the Miami Heat.)

———

My pursuit of education and advancement through seminars and management programs fueled my desire for new challenges. In my ten years as regional vice president of engineering and operations, I'd been responsible for managing the engineering, surveillance, and operations of the broadband network for the Oklahoma region that delivered residential and commercial customer services. This included managing all outside plant maintenance, construction, engineering, network operations, and commercial service installation and repair. Under my leadership, our team upgraded the network for DOCSIS 3.0, upgrading over ten thousand miles of plant to 1 GHz. DOCSIS is "data over cable service interface specification," an international telecommunications standard that enables you to add high-bandwidth data transfer to an existing cable TV (CATV) system. My team also significantly improved network reliability, reducing outages by 55 percent and line problems by 25 percent. I co-led an enterprise-wide next-generation network operations transformation team focused on standardizing network operations and engineering functions to improve product deployment, time-to-market, and customer experience.

After two category-five tornadoes struck Oklahoma within eleven days of each other, I supervised the engineering and operations teams during recovery operations. So, at fifty-one, I felt more than ready to take on a bigger role, something at a corporate O-level position at Cox Communications headquarters in Atlanta, Georgia.

I was also inspired by the success of one of my friends. When I first began working for Ameritech/Michigan Bell, I attended an intense training program in Illinois for high-potential engineers called PDOTS (planning, design, and operation of the telecommunications system). In the class, I became friends with a classmate from Ameritech/Illinois Bell named Liz Watson. She and I, along with Liz's boyfriend, Don Thompson, and a few others, would stay up at night playing bid whist. Over time, I grew close to the couple, hanging out with them, playing bid whist, going to clubs and restaurants in Chicago, and sleeping on the couch in their apartment.

Don and Liz were both engineering graduates from Purdue. One day, Don, who worked for Northrop but was unhappy with his job, told me he was taking a job at McDonald's.

I said, "You mean McDonnell Douglas, right?"

He said, "No, McDonald's." He'd been accepted into a management training program and was excited. Over time, Don and Liz got married, had two children, and moved to Denver, San Diego, and back to Illinois as his career progressed. I was energized by his success and in 2010, I attended the Executive Leadership Council (ELC) Annual Recognition Gala in New York, where Don received the organization's highest honor, the ELC Achievement Award. The ELC is the preeminent membership organization for the development of global black leaders. Don's career skyrocketed and in 2012, he was named CEO of McDonald's! Don grew up in the Cabrini-Green housing project. The moral of his story: do what you love and love what you do. Don inspired me. If he'd continued to slog through his days at Northrup and avoided the risk he took by changing industries, he might never have hit his stride and worked his way up to lead the one of the largest companies in the World. (Surprisingly, he retired in 2015 after an amazing twenty-five-year career.)

In 2013, after interviewing for a couple of key roles, I was promoted to vice president of national network operations. I had responsibility for managing an organization of nearly five hundred employees, providing strategic direction and leadership for the support and maintenance of current and future technologies (voice, high-speed data, video, WiFi) for residential and commercial customers. I'd now play a key role in identifying new technologies, tools, and processes to improve operations of the NOC and regional NOCs, enhancing network availability and reliability of critical applications and platforms while also reducing unit costs.

This provided me with an opportunity to gain experience managing an operation enterprise-wide. I received an attractive salary, bonus, and long-term incentive pay. The relocation benefits included Cox purchasing the house in Edmond, which allowed me to realize significant appreciation in the home's value, and expenses for the move to Atlanta. I attended the Cox Executive Leadership Development Program (ELDP) at the University of Georgia, which further sharpened my management skills.

I felt like an MVP. I was doing great work, reaping substantial rewards, and I was at the top of my game. To reward ourselves, in 2014, Renita and I built a winter home in north Phoenix, Arizona, a city I have always enjoyed for its spectacular mountain views, awesome fall and spring weather, resort spas, and—naturally—the Grand Canyon.

This new career success was short-lived. I found the culture and teamwork at the corporate headquarters to be very different from life in the field. While the larger cable companies were consolidating and growing customers, Cox had a stagnant or shrinking customer base. After I'd been working in my new role for about two years, I heard rumblings that my department was looking to make changes, possibly reducing leadership positions. When I mentioned this to a good friend, she encouraged me to hire an employment attorney; fortunately, I did. The attorney negotiated a fair and generous exit package, and I re-signed during a department reorganization.

The change brought unexpected stress to our life. When I closed the separation deal with the company, Renita was traveling internationally for work. On her return flight connection in Dallas, she called to ask how things were going. I told her I would fill her in when she returned home, but she insisted I tell her *right now*. I told her. She was very shaken and worried. I didn't tell the children right away; I eventually told them about two weeks later. I knew their reactions would differ widely. My oldest daughter, Lauren, was worried; she knows how tough it can be to find a comparable job in a weak economy. My second daughter, Rachel, wasn't worried at all; she knows I've overcome long odds my entire life and have always found a way to succeed. My son, Brian, the youngest child, based his reaction on how I was reacting; if I wasn't worried, he wasn't going to worry.

Fortunately, I'm very knowledgeable in matters of personal finance. Remember, I was doing the family finances at age eight! Over the years, I'd been saving for retirement, college tuitions, and unexpected events. I also owned two homes and had no other debts. Between my savings, vested pension, and the severance package I received, I was well positioned for maintaining our lifestyle until such time I was working full-time again.

I spent the next twelve months focused on the family. Brian was entering his senior year in high school. I worked with him on his college admission and scholarship applications. He ended up receiving four scholarships, including the Fry Scholarship. I was also able to support Renita during her recovery from arthritis surgery; she was off work for six months. I had time to exercise daily. I eventually began consulting part-time and searching for a new job.

As an unemployed minority executive, I pursued several potential opportunities across the country with both established and start-up firms. I had numerous phone interviews, and went on several in-person interviews that took me to Stamford, CT; Atlanta, GA; Houston, TX; Denver, CO; Seattle, WA; Mountain View, CA; and Cincinnati, OH. I reached the offer stage with three of the firms. One company decided to hire an internal candidate instead. Another company had a management shake-up that put the position on hold indefinitely. The third company changed their deployment strategy and put the position on hold. I was disappointed initially, but when they later announced that they were halting their expansion plans and reducing staff, I realized that I had dodged a bullet.

Finding an executive-level position isn't easy. Consolidation in the cable and telecommunications industry had significantly reduced the number of executive-level positions in my field. They are few in supply and are typically filled by internal or younger candidates. Nevertheless, I was relentless and determined in my job search. I wasn't discouraged by the enormous challenge. I'd been overcoming obstacles and challenges all my life. Through my life experiences, I'd learned to be calm under pressure. I continued talking to recruiters and interviewing. One of my former employees passed along a recruiting contact. I followed up and eventually landed an executive position with Charter Communications, America's fastest-growing television, Internet, and voice company.

My new position was vice president of regional field engineering in Cincinnati. I was fifty-four. Charter had just completed its acquisition of Time Warner Cable and Bright House Networks. While I couldn't have planned it that way, the new firm and position proved to be the most satisfying and enjoyable of my entire professional career. The job was a great match for my background, skills, and interests, and with a company led by some very smart and savvy cable veterans. Charter's focus was on growth, execution, and delivering strong customer service results.

Relocating to another city and state was a big undertaking, but by then I had extensive experience in moving, which helped to minimize the stress. Based on my experience, we decided to rent a house as we waited for our home in Marietta, Georgia, to sell. Meanwhile, we could figure out where we wanted to live in the Cincinnati metro area.

To celebrate the new job, Renita and I went to Las Vegas to see the Mariah Carey "#1 to Infinity" Show at The Colosseum in Caesar's Palace. We have been Mariah Carey fans ever since her first single, "Vision of Love." The amazing show and great weekend getaway helped smooth the bumps out after a rough year. It also helped crystallize another life lesson:

A Walk Is the Same as a Single

It's satisfying to hit that perfect pitch in the sweet spot and knock one out of the park. It's much less so to get on base because the pitches aren't hitting the strike zone. A walk isn't a failure to hit; it's another way to advance. Never stop competing.

Top of the Ninth

I hadn't known how things were going to work out when I left Cox; I just knew things would work out for the best at some point. The employment attorney I hired ensured that the company treated me fairly, so I didn't have to worry about whether the company was going to look out for the best interests of me and my family. Our faith is challenged during difficult times. I had to keep the faith and assure my family that everything was going to be just fine. That included getting my son settled into college and paying for my oldest daughter's wedding.

As Renita and I continue on our life's remarkable journey, we often think about what is next for us—right around the corner as well as longer-term considerations. When we retire, we'd like to have another home in an area of the country that is diverse and progressive, but Renita has always wanted to return to Texas, too. We are fortunate enough that we can begin planning our future retirement home in the next few years.

As it is for many Americans, a large part of our planning for retirement means deciding how long we will both work. Fortunately, we are among the small percentage for whom this will be more a matter of choice than of necessity. We have employer pension annuities and Social Security to sustain us. We've made wise investments over the years, too, but perhaps the one that will pay the biggest dividends is our investment in ourselves: exercising and maintaining a healthy lifestyle will pay big dividends in our golden years. Medical insurance coverage is always a major concern as people age. The future of the Affordable Care Act is very important to us.

We want to travel and enjoy life. We have both worked very hard since we were young. Working hard and providing for the children and their futures has dominated my life over the last thirty years. Retirement will be a balance of enjoying ourselves now but maintaining and managing the necessary resources for the future. The good news is that my children all possess a great education, have excellent careers, and are very independent. While they will always appreciate a little financial help or an unexpected gift, they aren't dependent upon us for financial assistance.

As important as planning is to success, there are always surprises. As I reflect on my professional career over the last thirty years, I see that my greatest strength has been my ability to adjust my swing to match the pitcher, and to stay ahead of the count more often than not. I had to recover from two major unexpected and eye-opening job events: the failure of the startup Birch Telecom in the dot-com crash, and my unplanned departure from Cox just a few years ago. Both times I kept working, doing what I could to keep going, while planning my next move.

You might think that my "golden parachute" from Cox hardly counts as a crisis. It's true that it wasn't a life-altering job loss: I wasn't the sole breadwinner, nor was I barely hanging on from paycheck to paycheck. But you have to realize that the higher the level or position you achieve on the career ladder, the greater the employment risk. Finding a highly compensated position takes more time than finding something that's "just a job." You could be out of work for a long time if you choose to wait for a job that's equivalent to or above the level of your previous position.

For most people, losing a job is a very difficult situation to overcome. Some never recover from a job loss. Unemployment involves financial and mental stress, and tosses uncertainty into the best laid plans. It's potentially damaging to your ego; being "downsized," let go, or outright fired can cause you to question your self-worth. In a country where the first small-talk question people toss at you is, "What do you do?" being without a job requires a strong mind, a strong support system, and a strong desire and determination to succeed. As Winston Churchill is rumored to have said, "Success is not final, failure is not fatal: it is the courage to continue that counts."

———

In many respects, I've lived an amazing life. I've been able to overcome some major obstacles and unexpected challenges and achieve a modest level of success. Most people who meet me assume that I was raised in a middle- or upper-middle-class family by two college-educated, working-professional parents. Some people mistakenly assume that I have somehow been lucky in life. I find it ludicrous that someone would assume luck was the underlying reason for success rather than hard work and determination.

My life began with humble beginnings and significant challenges, including the tragic loss of my father, the protracted and preventable death of my mother, and the violent death of my brother. We lived month-to-month financially on government assistance, and I started managing our family finances before I'd even hit puberty. As I grew up, I had to make my own way, including figuring out how to pay for college—and for everything else. I often said that if I didn't work, I couldn't eat: I forced myself to be completely self-sufficient, buying my own car, buying my own clothes, and putting a roof over my head. I have experienced my fair share of life's ups and downs, but how I responded in difficult situations is what counted ultimately, and determined how tough it was to bounce back.

Overcoming obstacles at different stages in my life has made me resilient and determined. I could have easily given up several times. Many people expected me to. But giving up is not what I wanted, and not what I expected of myself. Everyone's resiliency to hardships is not the same. One person's inner strength may be very different from another's. Mine was conditioned early on to be strong. Even though my parents were no longer living, I wanted to make them proud. They instilled strong family values that sowed the seeds of success that grew and blossomed within my sister and within me over the years. I wanted the world to know that Ossip Sr. and Birdie Mitcham raised good, loving, and successful children.

Perhaps their loving presence is why I always wanted my own children and family. Fatherhood made me a better person. I would not be the person I am today without being blessed with my children, Lauren, Rachel, and Brian. And even though my first marriage ended in divorce, I learned from the experience. My second marriage has been very happy and fulfilling.

With the help of wise mentors and role models, I learned how to position myself for a career in corporate America—taking advantage of internship opportunities in college and obtaining a BSEE degree and an MBA. Education changed the trajectory of my life, and positioned me to take important steps toward my career goals. Sometimes these were steps forward, sometimes they were sideways, and a few times steps back, but I always kept moving.

I took chances with my professional career, moving several times for new opportunities, switching companies more than a few times. Success changed my socioeconomic status and entrusted me with the important responsibility of being a good role model not just for my children but for others in the work force. I took seriously my obligation to help others, especially minorities and the traditionally disenfranchised, and to guide members of the next generation through activities like mentoring.

I don't know what the future holds for me; my story is still being written. What I do know is that I am happy and ahead in the count. I'm an optimist; I always believe that things will work out, even if you don't know what success looks like at the time.

You have to believe in yourself, even when no one else does. Ask yourself, "What is the alternative?" Keep working toward a goal, doing the right things until everything works out. That is what I call faith: believing in an ideal when you don't know how or when it will materialize. It reminds me of a line from the movie *The Preacher's Wife*: "Just because you can't see the air doesn't keep you from breathing."

Detroit is a perfect example of having faith and bouncing back; the city continues to get back up after being knocked down. After watching my beloved Detroit Tigers win the World Series in 1968 and 1984, I'm looking forward to seeing them win another World Series. The 2016 Detroit Tigers season was the team's 116th season. They finished the season in second place in the American League Central division, with an 86–75 record. Just as the success of the Tigers in 1968 helped the torn and divided city to rally together behind them after the 1967 race riot, another World Series championship could strengthen the city's resurgence.

Back in the early 1970s, entrepreneur Emily Gail coined the slogan "Say nice things about Detroit!" Well, there are plenty of nice things to say about Detroit. Detroit's commercial property and downtown business district is rebounding slowly and steadily. Three casinos and adjacent hotels buttress the downtown area, enhancing the city's draw

as a destination for conventions and conferences. Campus Martius, headquarters of Compuware and Quicken Loans, is "packed with performance stages, moveable chairs, lush greenery, and multiple restaurants. In the summer, there's an urban beach, and in the winter, there's a skating rink that draws tens of thousands." [19] Developers estimate that the greater downtown needs three to five thousand new rental apartments—enough to keep construction crews busy for the next few years at least.[20] The automotive industry's resurgence and new interest in the city by technology companies is helping to bolster markets there as memories of the city's bleak past fades away. And my beloved Tigers (and the Lions) delight crowds of sports fans in their state-of-the art stadiums.

Life is like baseball.
1. You will not hit every pitch.
2. Make the most of the balls you hit.
3. Keep your eye on the ball!

Every At-Bat is a New Chance

---

19. https://dirt.asla.org/2016/06/24/the-resurgence-of-downtown-detroit/.

20. http://www.freep.com/story/money/business/michigan/2016/01/02/detroit-midtown-downtown-gilbert/78027012/.

www.ingramcontent.com/pod-product-compliance
Lightning Source LLC
LaVergne TN
LVHW051808080426
835513LV00017B/1861